ABOUT CHRIST

WILLIAM TEMPLE

*The Archbishop's lectures in 1921 and 1925
on 'The Universality of Christ' and
'Christ's Revelation of God' reprinted
with a preface by the Archbishop of York
and an essay by J. Eric Fenn*

SCM PRESS LTD
BLOOMSBURY STREET LONDON

also by William Temple

CHRISTIAN FAITH AND LIFE

Addresses in the Mission to Oxford 1931

(Reissued as SCM Paperback 1963)

This Edition 1962
Second impression 1963
© SCM Press Ltd 1962
Printed by Charles Birchall & Sons Ltd
Liverpool & London

CONTENTS

PREFACE (1962)

by the Archbishop of York

One of the signs of great teaching is that, in its essentials, it does not date. An instance of this is to be found in the commentaries of J. B. Lightfoot on the Pauline Epistles. On certain linguistic points they are, of course, out of date, for Lightfoot could not anticipate the findings of the *ostraca* and *papyri* whose relevance for the New Testament was to be evaluated soon after his death. But, in the main, these commentaries are still full of invaluable material for the student of the New Testament.

These lectures by William Temple to students were given in 1921 and 1925. Yet they are still alive and completely relevant. They deal with the big things of God and of our faith, and have a living message for our day. It is for this reason that I welcome their republication. I hope they will be read widely, both within the student world and outside it.

DONALD EBOR:

FORTY YEARS LATER

by J. Eric Fenn

THE year 1921 must seem to most people about as remote as the Flood, and 1925 little better. The inter-war years, and even such names as Mussolini and Adolf Hitler, are for most of those in their twenties merely reminiscences of an older generation. Why, then, republish two series of lectures, the first given in 1921 and the second in 1925?

When Dr Temple, Bishop of Manchester from 1921, gave the first four of these lectures in Glasgow he was speaking to a section of the student population which was probably unique. Universities and colleges were filled with ex-servicemen, back from the First World War. They were an older generation, many were battle-scarred, and most had known the responsibilities of command. Those who were interested in religion at all were seriously and responsibly interested. 2,448 students went from the colleges to the Glasgow conference, organized by the Student Christian Movement, and they flocked to hear Temple's lectures.[1] Largely as a result of this conference, the SCM in Britain was able to mobilize and direct the idealism and determina-

[1] *Cf.* T. Tatlow, *The Story of the SCM*, p. 696: 'This was the only occasion on which I have seen hundreds of university men and women running like hares to get into a religious meeting. The church where Temple spoke was packed daily, and he was at his very best.'

tion of some of the best among the survivors of the
slaughter of 1914-18—to the lasting benefit of Church and
Nation.

By 1925, when Temple gave the second series at another
large SCM conference in Manchester, the situation had
already begun to change. The ex-service generation had
almost gone and boys and girls were again arriving at the
universities straight from school. The mixture of older and
younger students was an uneasy one, and a good deal of the
edge had gone from the enthusiasm. Once again, however,
Temple's lectures were well attended and effective.

Taken together, these seven lectures represent at a very
high level a reasoned presentation of the Christian Faith,
in conscious relation to other faiths, made to intelligent and
educated young people forty years ago. That alone might
provide sufficient reason for reprinting them; yet they are
of much more than historical interest. It is remarkable how
much that was said in so different a context is still directly
relevant to-day: remarkable, because the intellectual
climate, in almost every respect, has suffered so violent a
change since those days.

In 1921, the philosophers were still, for the most part,
living in the world in which Temple had been brought up
and in which he was at home. He could speak, as in these
lectures or in *Mens Creatrix* (1917), of philosophy as the
quest for wholeness and for ultimate truth, and know that
he would be understood: for neither existentialism nor
the linguistic analysis had, as yet, made any serious inroad
into what seemed a settled and permanent tradition. Moreover, in 1921, nobody in England, and probably only one
or two people in Scotland, knew of the publication of a

commentary on the Epistle to the Romans by an unknown Swiss pastor named Karl Barth; certainly nobody had any inkling of the ferment which this book would arouse in Continental theology, or any premonition of its delayed action in Great Britain. A few were deeply concerned about a much earlier book by Albert Schweitzer, *The Quest of the Historical Jesus*; but, after all, contacts between British scholars and their Continental colleagues had been broken by the War and it took some time to restore them. It was only then that the ferment began which altered the whole climate in which men must think.

The change has been no less remarkable in the field of natural science, for in 1921 Rutherford had not yet succeeded in 'splitting the atom', even though his classical experiments were but the faint beginnings of what we now know on a gigantic scale. Most of the scientific achievements which we now take for granted were undreamed of, except in the fertile brain of Mr H. G. Wells; and the philosophy of science was still largely concerned with issues left over from the previous century. The conception of the universe, and the understanding of the very nature of science itself, have changed almost out of knowledge.

While Archbishop of York (1929-42) and of Canterbury (1942-44) Temple himself became aware of an almost complete break between his way of thought and that of younger theologians both inside and outside of the Church of England. He was conscious of an increasingly difficult problem of mutual understanding which appeared to be without solution. It is a further tribute to his greatness that he retained the loyalty and respect of younger men, in spite of this difficulty of communication.

It is perhaps too early to assess this change in perspective. It may be that what seems to have been a radical break with the tradition of the nineteenth and early twentieth centuries will turn out to be a mere hesitation, taking stock by asking after the meaning of the words we use when we are trying to think and speak philosophically; and this may well have been long overdue. Linguistic analysis and existentialism are certainly reminders that ultimate reality cannot be reached by constructing a 'world view', or a nicely balanced philosophical system such as the nineteenth century sought after. Similarly, the impact of Karl Barth reminds us that revelation may never be taken for granted, but is always miracle; always, therefore, disturbing to any established theological or philosophical system, however deeply cherished. What is certain is that the world of 1921 was, in every respect, more different from that of today than it was itself different from the world of 1881, when William Temple was born.

It has become depressingly usual in intellectual Christian circles to regard the 1920's as a kind of desert or stagnant pool of 'liberalism', dangerous to theological health and without hopeful egress; a period when the young were encouraged to essay the fatal art of 'Kingdom-building', which all too often became a mere battering of heads against brick walls; and when the prevailing mood was one of reckless optimism, unrelated to the stern facts, whether of a recalcitrant world or of the 'Dialectical Theology'. This view is, perhaps, less common today than it once was; but that it was never generally true will be evident to anyone who reads what Dr Temple was saying in these lectures and meditates on the fact that literally thousands of young men and women listened eagerly and were deeply impressed. The clear, unambiguous affirmation of the Divinity of Christ; the carefully balanced doctrine of God and exposition of His relation to man and the world; the categorical refusal of any syncretistic solution of the conflict between Christianity and other faiths—all these represent a kind of balanced realism which, if it lacks some of the sharp antitheses and paradoxes of more recent writers, is certainly very far removed from the views attributed to the generation which was most deeply influenced by William Temple.

There is, for instance, a great deal in the lecture on *The Comparative Method* which is of urgent importance for us today, particularly when we are threatened by two dangers: that of pushing Jesus Christ into the past and leaving Him there, as an interesting spiritual phenomenon, and that of retreating from the complications of the historical method altogether and taking refuge in a new obscurantism. It may be that the central problem confronting the Church in our generation is how to bring home to men the contemporary, present reality of Christ without sacrificing the indubitable gains of historical and comparative study. And here Temple has important things to say, particularly in his lecture on *Christ the Complete Revelation*, taken in conjunction with the three lectures on *Christ's Revelation of God* (themselves a distillation of the 1924 book *Christus Veritas*). What he has to say may be summarized in this quotation from a passage in which he deals with the relation of Christianity to other faiths: 'The one thing we are bound to require, as it seems to me, is that men shall say that this Christ is very God, not for the sake of doing honour to Jesus of Nazareth—He did

not claim honour for Himself—but because every thought
of God which is not in accord with the character of Jesus
Christ is idolatry, a false image of God; and the more we
dwell upon it, the worse it will be for us.'

It is still true for us, as it will remain true for every
generation, however revolutionary the changes in the
world may be and however the categories of thought may
alter, that the central assertion of Christianity, that 'God
was in Christ, reconciling the world to Himself', remains
the rock on which we may either stumble or build. We live
today in a rootless world. The sheer pace and scope
of change, the deep precariousness of daily existence, the
heavy question-mark over the future, all combine to persuade us that there can be no final wisdom and no continu-
ing city. The results are only too apparent in the eager
discarding of moral conventions and moral standards associated with the past, and the lack of any real understanding
between young and old. The present is all that men can be
sure of. But this, if they could but see it, is an unveiling
of the human situation as it has always been and always
must be: we cannot be sure of anything except that we
are, and that one day we shall not be. The question
is whether there is another unveiling, equally present and
even more disturbing, the unveiling of God in His judgment and mercy. And this is the Christian message—to us
no less than to our predecessors and to those who may come
after us: for what is unveiled in Jesus Christ is present
reality, and therefore supremely relevant to our existence.

It is because this is made so abundantly clear in these lectures that they have something urgent to say to us, as urgent and as arresting as when they were first spoken.

THE UNIVERSALITY OF CHRIST
CHRIST
1921

I

THE COMPARATIVE METHOD

My subject, plainly, is of vast dimensions, and I want first to say a word or two about the general plan which I propose to follow. It is quite clear that so great a subject as that which has been allotted to me can only be dealt with, in a course of four lectures, by the deliberate selection of one line of approach and then by an outline treatment. It is therefore quite likely that my method may not be one which supplies a direct answer to the questions with which you have come to these meetings. But I have chosen the line which seems to me most fruitful in suggesting answers to the particular questions that in my experience are the commonest in men's minds and are the most urgent in my own. So today I am going to speak about those two methods of study which have come recently into the field of inquiry, one of them well established, the other by this time also having put its claims beyond question—the historical and the comparative methods. To follow them in detail would be impossible, and we will merely consider what they are capable of achieving and what lies beyond their province. Tomorrow I hope to speak about the general conception of a universal religion: how far it is philosophically credible that there should be such a religion at all? and if it is credible, what are the requirements which we shall have to make of any religion if it is to be regarded as a claimant for the place of the one universal religion? After that we shall come to the central theme: Is Christianity qualified to meet these requirements? Is the religion of Christ the one universal religion? In the fourth lecture our question will be: If in principle it appears that the religion of Christ is qualified to be the one universal religion, does it work out in practice as satisfying the need? On the way we shall raise, and suggest answers to, a large number of questions that are most commonly in the minds of thinking people at the present time. Further, I have been specially asked to try to treat the subject from the philosophical and intellectual point of view, and therefore, in order that we may achieve something on that line, I have deliberately excluded the more emotional side of religion, and with it a great deal of what is more important in the spiritual life of religion. I am anxious to say this at the outset, because otherwise an attempt to handle the matter as the intellect is bound to handle it may seem extraordinarily dry and dull and lifeless.

The study of religion, like nearly every other study, was profoundly modified during the nineteenth century by the introduction of the historical method. The historical method was not itself a novelty in the strict sense. It is to be found in all ages when men have pursued any inquiry in the strictly scientific spirit, and it is markedly prominent in Aristotle. Aristotle subjected the religious beliefs of the Greek philosophers before his time to a treatment by the historical method extraordinarily similar to that which modern thinkers apply to various formulations of religious beliefs, including the beliefs of Christianity. But there was another great tradition which came from Greece, and which in this respect impressed itself upon the mind of the Church. That was the tradition of Platonism. There can be no doubt that the Platonic method is rather hostile to any free and full use of the historical method, because the thinker who is very much akin to Plato in temper of mind will always be so concerned about the eternal and the unchanging that he is rather impatient of any discussion of development, and exceedingly impatient of any suggestion that what he believes to be eternal and unchanging is itself only a phase in a long process of development which has to be carried further.

The contrast in the case of the two Greek philosophers is strongest in the sphere of politics, where Aristotle has a quite clear conception of the processes by which one form can give rise to another, and therefore how progress can be guided, while Plato has no suggestion for the initiation of the ideal state except the half humorous one, that all citizens over ten years of age should be banished and the others trained in the national nurseries by a philosopher king. That is what happens when you leave the historical method out.

Now the Church very naturally adopted the Platonic traditions in this matter. The Church was concerned with eternal truth. It was perfectly sure that in the life and work of Christ the eternal truth had been given to it by God, and hardly anyone paused to consider whether any of the particular ways in which, either in previous ages or in the age contemporary with any given theologian, that truth had been expressed was part of the eternal and unchanging, or was merely a shape into which it was cast by the mental habits of a particular age. Therefore in religion the historical method was for a long time practically ruled out, and it was not until the eighteenth century, I think, that it began to be permanently introduced. Then, with the general rise of the scientific habit of mind in other fields of life which had come with the Renaissance, there came an application of the historical method to the field of religion also. As we all know, however, it was through the development of biology, and particularly the application of the doctrine of evolution in biology (although the doctrine of evolution was already perfectly familiar before the biologists took it up) that men's minds were generally so transformed that they became unable to think of any belief or convention or institution except in the terms of its historical origin. During the nineteenth century that point of view became steadily more and more deeply rooted, so that anyone who really thought about anything was always thinking under the guidance of the question: What is the origin of this thing, and through what processes has it passed from its origin to its present state?

First we are bound to acknowledge that there is immense value in this method. There is a value in it as applied to all human institutions, because the human race is in process of growth and of movement, and everything which bears the impress of human nature must reflect this predominant fact about the human species, that it is moving on, whether biologically or not, certainly morally and politically, from stage to stage—not always in progress; sometimes in retrogression—but always in movement. Politically it is found that there is hardly any chance of understanding the problems with which we are confronted unless we study their historical origin. Those who are particularly concerned about the reform of the economic structure of society have found themselves driven more and more to inquire into the processes—the very lengthy processes—by which society as we know it today has reached its present stage. There is no means of understanding a thing as it is except through knowledge of what it has been.

There has been a particular gain from the application of this method to that progress in the knowledge of God of which we have the record in the Bible. So long as men ignored the fact of historic growth, and tended to equate all periods of human life and thought in spiritual value, they were confronted by problems, especially in the ethics of some parts of the Old Testament, to which there was no solution. On the other hand, once you are familiar with the thought of progress from stage to stage as being fundamental to the method whereby it has pleased God to lead mankind into a fuller knowledge of Himself, then it becomes not a difficulty, but exactly what we should expect in advance, when we discover that in the earlier periods men had a very partial capacity to receive the Divine truth, which God is always offering to the full extent of that capacity. And so, as we watch the Old Testament, one of the plainest marks upon the face of it is this, that as men lived as far as they were able in fellowship with God, they came to understand more and more His unchanging truth and nature. It is not that He has changed or altered His message to men's souls; it is that you cannot pass through a pipe a greater volume than that pipe is fashioned to contain, and if the receptivity of the human soul is limited, then the amount of Divine truth which it can receive is limited thereby. It is as men live loyally in the fullest light they have that they become more capable of receiving more light. It is not that God changed, but that men's understanding of Him changed.

One of the things that the historical method will do for the Christian at once is to bring him to say that just because Jesus Christ is the crown of the revelation He is also its criterion, and that everything which in other revelations is not compatible with what has come to us in Christ, must be, without any hesitation at all, attributed to the human medium through which the revelation came, and not to its Divine source. Thereby an enormous host of difficulties are swept away without in the smallest degree endangering the belief that God was indeed communicating His truth to men from age to age, they receiving it as they were able to receive it.

But there is a difficulty which at present I am not going to enter upon fully, because it will concern us later, although it arises immediately. The Christian, we say, adopting the historical method, is perfectly ready to affirm that our Lord, because He is the crown, is also the criterion of the revelation. But how can He be the crown? How can the perfect revelation be already given? How is it possible, if we believe in this constant movement of things—a movement which, as far as men are faithful to the highest things they know, is a movement of progress—how is it possible that centuries ago a complete revelation can have been given? That is going to be our main theme a little later, and I mention it now just to show I am not shirking it, but I do not deal with it at the moment because a full handling is only possible after consideration of the topics which we shall have before us tomorrow.

There is another great weakness in the historical method, if we do not supplement it, quite apart from any application to Christianity in particular. I said that the other tradition, the Platonic tradition, was more especially concerned with the eternal and unchanging, and it is only in the eternal and unchanging that the human mind, let alone the human spirit, can find rest. The whole impulse of science itself, when all is said and done, is to reach the truth, which is unalterable. We study a changing world, but we study it in order to find unchanging principles of its change. You study, let us say, biological evolution. No biologist is going to tell you he has actually observed and carefully noted, with details, the successive phases through which life has gone, and by which it has moved from its earlier stages to those we see it in now. The facts do not exist that would enable you to do such a thing. All that the biologist can do is to experiment with those forms of life which do exist now, observe the changes which ensue from particular treatment in mating and the like, and by means of inferences drawn from such experiments and observations go back to such scanty relics of the earlier forms of life as happen to be available and see whether they will fit into the scheme which the experiments have suggested. He presupposes that whatever principles govern changes at this moment are the same principles which governed changes ages back. His real concern is not with the detailed change from one phase to another, but with the unalterable and eternal principle. Evolution is a process of change, but the principle of evolution is an unchanging principle, and it is with this unchanging principle that even science, let alone religion, must be primarily concerned. It is possible so to exalt the historical method of study as to divert science itself from its natural and proper object. It is possible so to concentrate the mind upon the movement and the flux of things that you are left with no permanent principles at all, and, therefore, with no means of studying or obtaining real knowledge of the movements and the flux upon which you are concentrating attention.

If this is so in science, it is still more so in religion. No man of any spiritual experience would be prepared to tolerate the suggestion, for example, that when we set out to worship, we have first to ascertain the precise degree of perfection which God has now attained, in order that we may nicely adapt our praises. We know that the God before whom we humble ourselves is the God to whom Abraham spoke, if Abraham existed as an individual, which after all does not very much matter. Our knowledge of Him ought to be quite different from Abraham's, for we have received the illumination which was given to the world in Jesus Christ; but it is the same God with whom we are entering into communion. If it is not, then all the experience which seems to the religious man to be Divine fellowship is an illusion from top to bottom. Religion can never rest on the historical method. It will use it to illuminate the true contents of its own traditions. It will use it in order to know more fully the way by which God, in His mercy, has met the weakness of human nature from stage to stage, always leading steadily on to a fuller truth. But the religious man will never be content with the belief that there is no permanent truth, that there is no unchanging and eternal

God, and nothing at all except the changing state of human consciousness from generation to generation. If that turned out to be true, we should have to accept it; but in accepting it we should be laying religion once and for ever on one side.

The historical method has lately been supplemented by what is really only a form of the same treatment, but is generally distinguished as the comparative treatment. As the historical method compares the different periods of time, and tries to discover principles of growth connecting the earlier with the later, so the comparative method, without reference to time, studies the beliefs, the conventions, the institutions of the different religions, and compares one with another, trying to find principles which will unite them in some intelligible system. The comparative method in one sense has been very familiar in the Christian Church, and I think we have to admit there has been sometimes a definite abuse of it by Christians under the influence of their zeal. Sometimes it would seem that the mere difference between religion as they have known it and the beliefs with which they have come in contact in other countries has convinced them that if their religion is true, all others must be merely and simply false. There has been sometimes also a tendency to press with great force upon all the least admirable sides either of those other faiths or of the life which they have inspired, while the tendency in dealing with Christian countries has been to exalt the ideal elements and the best products. Of course, it is very tempting to any propagandist of any belief always to produce the best product of that which he advocates and compare it with the least desirable results of possible substitutes. I think it cannot be denied that at missionary meetings that has been sometimes done.

One great gain that the scientific use of the comparative method in religion has brought us is the duty of genuine reverence for other men's beliefs. To reverence them is not at all the same thing as to accept them as necessarily true; but whatever thoughts any human soul is seeking to live by, deserve the reverence of every other human soul; and the comparative method of religion is the intellectual expression of that belief. It rests upon the conviction that everything that men believe deeply is worth studying sympathetically and thoroughly.

Nowadays, on the whole, the abuse of this method seems to me to be commoner in anti-Christians than in Christians —a great deal commoner. We have the failures of Christian civilization impressed upon us and the lofty ideals of some, for example, of the great Eastern faiths. That is no more satisfactory, either as science or as a means to the promotion of religious truth, than the other process of which I was speaking a moment ago. We have got to be definitely on our guard lest in our Christian desire to be charitable to those who profess another belief than ours, we are led to accept too light-heartedly their account of their own faith, in contrast with the practical working of ours. We must insist that when we talk about ideals, we will talk about ideals in both cases, and that if we talk about practice, we will talk about practice in both cases. We must not compare the Christian ideal with the practice of Mohammedanism, or the ideal of Buddhism with the practice of Christianity. Neither is legitimate. We must compare practice with practice, ideal with ideal, and only so can we go forward, either on a scientific basis or on one of justice.

The strength of this comparative method lies in the respect for other men's convictions. Its weakness, equally with that of the historical method, is that it is not itself capable of establishing truth. No amount of study of the various religions in comparison with one another will enable you to determine the truth of any or all of them. It will only enable you to determine that one is better than the other. It would not follow that it was true. Its proper use would seem to me to be rather this, that we desire to seek the best that there is in all faiths and then to see whether or not in that faith which we have ourselves received, whatever it be, there is already contained the elements of value which we have discovered elsewhere. If not, then if that element seems to us to be genuinely true and valuable, let us try to incorporate it. If it is already there, let us learn from those others to develop more fully what was always part of our own tradition, though we have first seen it because of their emphasis upon it.

No one individual and no group of individuals has exhausted the resources of the Christian faith. Indeed I suppose that at no one period has the whole universal Church been continually realizing the whole truth of Christianity, even as men have actually known it. Most of us live by a comparatively few articles of our professed creed. One of the best ways of strengthening spiritual life and of realizing the elements already present in our tradition, but to which we have hardly attended, is by the study of comparative religions, as it is commonly called, though it ought to be called the comparative study of religions. This will best help us by enabling us to see where are the weaknesses in our personal or corporate religious life, which can be supplied by any element which we find to be developed to great fulness in other faiths. That is a good practical and valuable function, and different from the function of ascertaining truth. It may illuminate the search for truth, but it can never conclude it.

This leads me further to say something about the whole point of view which is involved in any great emphasis upon the historical or comparative methods. They have their place by all means; we cannot do without them; we must practise them; but it is also perfectly true that they concern themselves mainly with what *men* have thought and are thinking, and what we are concerned about in the spiritual life is not what *men* have thought and are thinking, but what *God* is and what *God* wills.

No doubt it is true that in intercourse with saintly people of all races we develop our knowledge of what God is and wills, but our concern must always be with God and not with man. Where is the emphasis in the Creed? Is it, *I* believe in God? Or is it, I believe in *God*? There is no doubt where the answer of all wholesome religion lies. The fact that I believe is of very little consequence to anyone except myself. The thing which is important is that there is a God to believe in. There is a story of a young lady who asked Dr Jowett: 'Oh, Master, do tell me—What do you think about God?' to which the Master replied: 'That, my dear young lady, is a very unimportant question; the only thing that signifies is what He thinks about me.' In all our efforts to study religious life, whether in our own or in other forms of faith, and to build up our conscience, our character, even to determine our form of service, if these things once get into the first place, the whole religious life is wrecked; you have got away from the one reality—God, and are centring upon your own feelings and activities. I remember hearing a real master of the spiritual life, Father Kelly, once saying: 'There used to be a thing called theology, which is the Greek for thinking about God. It is very old-fashioned now. Instead of that there is a thing called the philosophy of religion, which means thinking about your own nice feelings. It is very popular.' That is the danger of all these studies. In the New Testament, if it is true at all, we are face to face with God; if that is not true, the New Testament is written under an illusion from end to end. It would be a very interesting illusion, and it would be thoroughly worth while to study it, for it has produced great effects in the history of the world, but an illusion all the same. The men who wrote the books of the New Testament believed that in Jesus Christ, God Himself lived and walked about among them. 'The Word was made flesh and dwelt amongst us.' They start from there.

Well, you ask me how we are going to establish this matter of truth. That is the whole problem of philosophy. But just let me put this to you at any rate. The impulse of the human mind when it is seeking knowledge is exactly the same as the impulse of the human spirit when it is seeking goodness. It is an impulse towards totality. It is a desire to see things as a whole—to see one's self, if at all, only as an element in that whole. Logic is the science of this impulse towards totality. That is why Dr Bosanquet says that the spirit of logic is self-sacrifice. Just as in the moral and political world the one solution of our problems is always to see that, in the whole, we fit ourselves in the right place, fully doing our part in that place, but not claiming a place for which we are not fitted: so in the life of the mind the object is always to see one great entire system, which includes all the facts, each in its own place, so that together they constitute the totality which determines for them their function.

The system that is capable in this way of gathering up all the facts of experience in one single whole, co-relating them all together, must also be in its own governing principle one satisfactory to reason and therefore akin to the human mind. That is the philosophical claim, and there is no other test of truth, so far as I know, more satisfying than that.

While it is clear that this test of truth is never finally applicable, we are able to apply it in increasing measure as our experience develops; and as our knowledge grows it becomes more and more possible to see how the inorganic and the organic, the mental and physical worlds are all related in one single whole, governed by a spiritual principle. If that is so, we may claim to be on the way to truth.

Now it is perfectly plain that Christianity, whether in the New Testament or in the Church from that day to this, has never made a claim to be acknowledged chiefly on intellectual grounds, and therefore all such enquiries as we are engaged upon in this lecture can never be more than a preparatory clearing away of obstacles, opening up avenues of approach. Christianity is faith, not knowledge; and the two are not the same. The spiritual value depends upon its being faith. You have that faith when a man says: 'It would be so splendid if this were true that I will always live as if it were true.' That is faith, and its spiritual value depends on its intellectual uncertainty. If once our faith became intellectually demonstrable, we should become higher or lower than the spiritual beings we are; but we should not have the same spiritual opportunity which is ours, the opportunity to stake our lives upon a noble hazard. Christianity comes with the claim to be the truth, and therefore to provide us with an all-embracing principle which will unite all parts of the universe in a complete totality. We are bound to go on using our minds to see whether that is so. We have got to think it out both in theory and in practice, and try to use it as a solution of our problems; and we should welcome what light the historical or comparative method has to bring. We are not to close our minds against any knowledge; for all knowledge is knowledge of the world, and the world is God's creation. If we are frightened of any kind of knowledge, it means that we have not really staked our lives on the belief that the world is God's and that God has made Himself known to us through Christ. It means that we are afraid that in the last resort, if we think about it hard enough, we shall find it is not true. An enormous amount of obscurantism finds its root in that kind of infidelity. If we stake ourselves mentally, as well as morally and spiritually, on the belief that it is the truth, we shall welcome all knowledge from all quarters, and confidently expect to find that whatever is true in other faiths is present, at least in germ, in the Christian faith, and that we have only to develop, under the stimulus of what we see in others, something which we have already inherited.

But Christianity, coming with this claim, is profoundly unaccommodating; it refuses to fit into a synthesis side by side with other systems, because it says it is the truth. When people say: 'Let us have a conference of all people of all religions, and find out what is good in each of them, and to see what is the real religion,' Christianity will have no interest in such a proposal. It will say: 'That will simply mean a watering down of the knowledge of God, which I have got, to suit others who have less. I dare not deny the things which have come to me through the Divine tradition and my own experience'; and similarly when any more up-to-date, modern-fashioned people say that the only charitable thing after all, and therefore the only Christian thing, is to suppose that all religions are equally true, and that the form which religion takes in different parts of the world is a matter of temperament—that it attacks Western people as Christianity, the Arabian as Mohammedanism, the Indian as Buddhism, the Chinese as Confucianism, and so on, and that all those are just variations of the one pure essential religion, we shall have to make two answers. First, if that is so, your precious religion is worth exactly nothing. It is only its different forms that give it meaning. The vague belief in God, which you find in the background of all the faiths of the world, is not a driving or regenerative power. It is simply no use at all. It will do nothing for you but give you what a certain kind of people call the 'cosmic consciousness', which is an element of religious experience, a sense of being at one with the great spirit which sustains the universe. But if you get no further than that, you will undergo a process which is perpetually occurring to students of all religions. You will transform what is in its essence spiritual and moral into something purely aesthetic. But there is this supreme difference between the spiritual and the merely aesthetic; the aesthetic experience lays no obligation upon conscience.

You can go to a concert and enjoy a symphony of Beethoven, and be elevated in feeling to the seventh heaven; and yet when you go out you do not feel any more charitable to the people in the 'bus you go home in; on the other hand you find them more intolerable than ever. And if that is all you are going to get out of the 'cosmic consciousness', and there is nothing else beyond it, you have taken the whole strength out of religion. Christianity was proscribed under the Roman Empire because it refused to take its place as one of the tolerated faiths. 'No,' it said 'ours is the true religion.' It was almost impossible in those days of conflict for the early Christians to go on, and explain that no doubt each of the other religions embodied some part of the whole truth which Christianity possessed. That is a point of view which is practically impossible in the actual heat of a bitter and persecuting conflict. But the claim of Christianity is not that it is one among a number of religions, all of which are good, each for a different set of people, nor indeed that it is primarily a drug for men's diseases at all, in which case we might suppose that there would be different drugs for different diseases; it claims that it is the truth about this world in which we live, and that from it and through it alone can you find in any fulness the knowledge of the God who made and who rules the world, and is guiding it to the fulfilment of His own purpose.

2

IS A UNIVERSAL RELIGION
POSSIBLE?

YESTERDAY we were considering two closely related methods of study applied to human religion: the historical, which is a comparison of what men have believed and experienced at different dates; and the comparative, which is a comparison as a rule of what men believe and experience at the present day in different places. Both of them, as we saw, had this mark; they are concerned with religion on its psychological side. They are concerned with religion as an activity of the human soul. And when we are taking steps to strengthen our devotional life or to commend our faith to those who do not at present accept it, we are bound to take notice of these psychological conditions. In strengthening the devotional life we have to understand what our own condition is in order that we may wisely handle it. We have to understand the kind of stimuli to which we react and so forth. In exactly the same way, if we want to commend our faith to other people, we must know the working of their minds sufficiently to realize which are the points that they can most easily apprehend first, so that having, as it were, got their footing in the world of faith, they may gradually make their own way in it, and become free of it as a whole. There is therefore this absolutely necessary place for the psychological study of religion.

But there is another danger about it, besides those which I mentioned yesterday, and which is more especially relevant to the theme that is to occupy us today. It is a danger, most clearly illustrated, I think, by Professor William James's well-known book, *Varieties of Religious Experience*. James virtually limits the term 'religious experience' to particular psychological occurrences, and moreover, to abnormal psychological occurrences. But the appeal of the Christian to religious experience as the warrant for his faith is not an appeal to particular ecstasies or to conversion or even to moments at one time or another of communion with the Divine—at least it is not to these exclusively. It is primarily to the whole experience of life as that is illumined and transformed by religious faith. Religious experience, as an evidence of the truth of religion, is not to be found mainly in momentary raptures, but rather in the whole outlook upon life which faith supplies, and the way in which experience from day to day perpetually vindicates that outlook. That is religious experience. It is not a particular episode in the midst of a non-religious experience; it is an experience of life and of the world which is religious through and through.

But this is a much more difficult thing for the psychologist to study. You can hardly deal with it by the method of *questionnaires*. And, having alluded to that method, let me remind you of its weakness. The American psychologists have put much stress on it; but it is misleading. If I were to send out an enormous number of questions to some thousands of people in England, taking them as far as I could at haphazard, asking them whether they had been converted at any particular moment in life, and whether their religious experiences of a particular kind were mostly connected with religious observances or independent of them, and so forth, a large proportion of the people who received that list of questions—the sanest and most ordinary sort of people—would immediately throw it into the waste-paper basket. The people who would answer would for the most part be people who have an interest in their own states. And therefore the whole method of trying to estimate the history and quality of religious life by means of *questionnaires* sent out broadcast tends to put the investigator into the hands of people who are spiritual valetudinarians. There can be no doubt that the psychological inquiry, most valuable as it has been, is vitiated to some extent by that fact. What you get is rather a kind of inventory of spiritual pathology than a trustworthy account of the spiritual processes of ordinary men and women. There is only one way in which we can escape from the inevitable untrustworthiness of all psychological forms of procedure. Use them by all means for illumination and supplement; but there is only one way of escaping from the bias which always besets those who give their special attention to states of human consciousness, and that is to turn away from the human interest in religion altogether towards the object—truth, reality, God.

And here let me remark incidentally that this is quite plainly the way of salvation now and always. It is the way of salvation in science, and it is the way of salvation in religion; for either in science or in religion, the first requirement is that a man should stop troubling very much about himself and concern himself with the object in hand. The scientist must not think of the result he wants from his experiments; he must look to see what really does happen. He has got to put all his predilections aside; he must not be primarily interested, for example, in providing evidence for the theories on which his reputation rests. He must be concerned with the facts and not with his desires; otherwise he will be no true scientist. And it is the same in religion. We must give ourselves over to the search for the real truth concerning God and His word. 'Thou hast made us for Thyself, and our souls are restless until they find rest in Thee.' It is only in the truth that they will find rest, and not in any devices of our contriving that may accord with what we suppose will bring us satisfaction.

In this objectivity of mind there is fellowship. So far as men are concerned with the object of their inquiry, they are brought together, for they have a common interest. As knowledge advances, all those who love knowledge can rejoice together. But if what the scientist is concerned about is not the increase of knowledge, but his own reputation, then, of course, he will be jealous when another makes a great discovery. The fellowship of science will be broken up. In the spiritual world it is the same. When we are all concentrated upon God and His service, we are brought into fellowship with one another; and we can rejoice in one another's achievements. But if what we are concerned about is primarily our individual spiritual state or, still worse, our spiritual reputation, then of course we begin to attend to what is ours distinctively, and so fall into separation from one another, and at last into antagonism. The way of salvation in science and in the spiritual life here, as in the case I mentioned yesterday, is still identical; it is that a man should forget all about himself in concentration on the object. The object, of course, is ultimate truth.

What is required of any conception which will warrant the attribution to it of ultimate truth is, as I said yesterday, that it be a totality—that it really include all the facts and include them as parts of one whole. It is worth while to remind ourselves how very much scientific study has helped us in the appreciation of this philosophic truth. People used once to ask with all seriousness the problems symbolically expressed in the question: If the earth stands on the elephant and the elephant stands on the tortoise, what does the tortoise stand on? That was a real problem; if all things fell downwards, they would all accumulate at the bottom; or if there is no bottom and they merely fall for ever, what is the actual difference between that and standing still? Science tells us that if the elephant stands on the tortoise, the tortoise stands on the elephant. If I stand on the earth, the earth stands on me; and there are people walking about in Australia, from our point of view, with their heads downwards.

It is all quite familiar, but very important. The system is not one in which you have one peg which is fixed somehow irretrievably, and then a number of links depending upon this, the whole chain depending at last upon the original peg. The system of reality, as science has revealed it to us in the physical universe, is a whole in which all the parts sustain one another in an articulated entirety. The method of the syllogism in logic, going down from certainty about a general proposition to the inferences that may be drawn from it, entirely misrepresents the nature of real truth. It was never a method of finding truth; it was a method of convincing opponents. The Greeks indulged in the noble and intellectual game of philosophic argument. Somehow it had to be settled who had won. The syllogistic logic stated the rules of the game, and made a decision as to the winner possible. It is not a method of science, but a method of argument. As such it is both valid and useful. We are rightly eager to employ it today; we want to say to the statesman, to the trader, to the editor: Are you a Christian? If so, you are committed to this or that particular action. That is a perfectly legitimate form of argument, but it is not a way of finding ultimate truth. It is a way in which you may find some particular truth. But the truth of any department of reality and of reality as a whole is to be found by building up all the factors of experience on which you can lay your hands in such a way that they dovetail into one another in a system which is both coherent and comprehensive.

Now this system, when you have got it, must contain its own explanation. When you look at it you must have no need to ask a further question. If you can still ask the question: If the world is so, why in the world should it be so? your truth is not ultimate. It does not give the final ground of all that is. How are you to reach a principle that does this? I am bound to be dogmatic; there is no time to work out possible alternatives to the only theory that seems to me to be conceivable. As far as our experience goes, I suggest to you, there is one principle and one principle only that we know which contains its own ground, and that is what we call purpose or will, which is spirit in action. When you find material objects with no sort of ascertainable purpose in their arrangement, you are not driven to ask how they came to be as they are, beyond such explanation as the purely physical causes can give you. You have a pile of boulders on the top of some mountain, and the geologist explains the processes by which, according to his system of inferences, these boulders came to be placed as they are now; and probably you are satisfied. You may raise the question why geological processes generally should be what they are. Most people do not trouble to do so, but it is perfectly legitimate; and the mind is then not satisfied by any further geologizing. But if you find stones so arranged in little heaps across a hill that they mark the easy way through the pass from one valley to another, you would be astonished to learn that this was entirely fortuitous, and that they had come there through geological processes only. On the other hand you are satisfied when you are told that they had been placed there by man for the intelligible purpose of marking a path, so that men might find their way in any mist. The moment that you arrive at something recognized by yourself as an intelligible ground determining the action of spirit in organizing matter in a certain way, the mind is in fact satisfied.[1]

That is, of course, why Plato said that the explanation of the universe is to be found at last in the Idea of Good; and he goes on—in that extremist manner, which makes one of his charms—to say, 'I want some philosopher to tell me whether the earth is round or flat by proving which it is better that it should be.'

Now I cannot wait to ask members of this audience whether in fact they have alternatives to the spiritual hypothesis whereby we may get a system of truth which

[1] Cf. Lecture I in my volume, *The Faith and Modern Thought*.

is inherently self-explanatory; and I must go on with the suggestion that in our experience, as a matter of fact, nothing else is self-explanatory except a will seeking good that we understand. Then we look at the world, and what do we find? We find it consists of a number of grades of being. It may be impossible to mark them off sharply from one another, but in their full development they are perfectly distinct—just as a boy of ten is a boy, and a man of fifty is a man, and an undergraduate is a hybrid. The law in its rough and ready way says that until you are twenty-one you are irresponsible, at any rate in certain relationships of life, but when you are twenty-one you are responsible. I did not find that my twenty-first birthday made any great difference to me in my moral and spiritual relationships; the only thing I noticed was that it was the first of my birthdays that nobody mentioned throughout the day. We need not mind this inability to draw a distinguishing line at any particular point. There is a difference between a baby in a cradle and a man in the fulness of his powers, though there may be a continuous process from one to the other. So in the world. You have a purely physical world, a world of brute Things, where we are able to assume that there is no purpose, no emotion, no thought, and even no sentience. That may not be philosophically quite correct, but we generally find it near enough for practical purposes; indeed if when you are playing golf you wonder if it will hurt the ball that you should hit it harder, you will find that it puts you off your game.

We begin with the level at which we suppose that there are none of those properties which we associate with life or with spirit. Then we come to the organic world, the

vegetable world. There is already life, although we generally suppose there is no sentience, thought, feeling, or purpose. You go on to the animal world, where there is certainly sentience, where there may be some degree of
thought (as, in the higher animals, there undoubtedly is),
and where in at least some animal races there is clear trace
of genuine purpose. Beyond that you have the human race
which possesses all those marks; and there may be further
developments still to come which will introduce elements
into the complexity of life as completely unknown to us as
our purpose for the moral unification of mankind is presumably unknown to the cabbage. When we look we see
further that each of these grades only achieves the fulness
of its own potentiality when it is possessed by the higher
grade. Nobody could ever deduce merely from the physical
properties of matter that it was capable of the infinite
delicacy of feeling that lies, let us say, in the artist's fingers.
It is only when we look at the lower grades from the point
of view of the higher and more complex that we begin to
understand the lower themselves. Again, we find that there
is a definite inter-action in those organisms where all the
grades are present together. I am not arguing the case now,
but it seems to me quite plain that there is definite inter-
action of spirit and matter, and that the state of our body
does undoubtedly affect, certainly our emotional condition,
very often even our purpose, while the whole point about
our purpose is that it is capable of directing our physical or-
ganism. In other words, life as we know it is sacramental
through and through, and from top to bottom. The principle of the whole system is that matter finds its real meaning when it is taken up into the purpose of spirit and is

utilized in that service, and that spirit only comes to itself, only expresses itself to other spirits but also only comes to full consciousness of its own meaning, when it possesses and directs matter. Spirit alone, with no material embodiment, accomplishes at least very little and perhaps nothing at all in this world; and that, no doubt, is why good intentions, which are of course purely spiritual, pave the way to hell. It is only when some concrete embodiment is found that spirit becomes real and active. In its own nature it is the function of matter to be dominated by spirit; it is the function of spirit to dominate matter. If that is so, and it is also true that in that spiritual principle you have one that is in itself self-explanatory, you have immensely strengthened the intellectual case for the hypothesis that spirit is the explanation of the world.

But if the explanation of the world—the principle that gives unity and coherence to the whole—is to be found in spirit, it must be in one spirit. A multiplicity of Beings cannot give unity to the whole of Being. This leads us to the supreme question of religion: If such a spirit exists, how is its nature to be known? It is not enough to say that the world is undoubtedly spiritual. It must be controlled by a spirit so conceived or known as to be adequate to account for our experience and also satisfactory to our moral aspirations, which are themselves among the facts of the universe. How is the ultimate truth to be known?

You will say at once that this is the precise object of philosophy. Yes, it is. But the method of philosophy, though perfectly sound in principle, will not serve our turn, for the simple reason that it requires eternity for its application. Philosophy will only bring you a sure knowledge of the ultimate truth when you have first of all acquired knowledge of the whole universe and have succeeded in constructing a theory adequate to the whole universe. It is at least probable that there are many kinds of existence of which we are quite incapable, in our present state, of becoming aware at all; so at least religious men of old have believed: 'Eye hath not seen, nor ear heard, neither hath it entered into the heart of man to conceive what good things the Lord hath prepared for them that love Him.' Human nature does not exhaust the capacity of the universe. There may even be forms of experience possible to other kinds of animals through sense organs which we do not possess, and from which we are shut out; and these facts have all got to be brought into your unified system before you have the right to close it. If you have a system of philosophy which is perfectly neat and compact on the basis of your own experience only, you can know for an absolute certainty that it is wrong. Therefore, while we ought to pursue the philosophical method so far as we can, perpetually seeking new knowledge and the co-relation of it with old knowledge, we cannot expect that we are going in our lifetime, or in the lifetime of our descendants for thousands of generations, or possibly in the existence of this planet at all, to find the ultimate truth by that method; and it is always possible that those elements which we cannot reach by any observations of ours may be among the most important for a correct inference.

The other method by which knowledge—or rather, let me say, apprehension—of the ultimate truth might come to us, is by revelation on the part of the Supreme Spirit whom we have found to be the most probable intellectual explanation of the world. If once you grant intellectually that there is such a Being, who may most fitly be thought of by us under the categories of will and purpose, then there is no difficulty whatsoever in the general conception that He may reveal Himself to man. On the contrary, there is a great deal of difficulty in the supposition that He will refrain from doing so. He has made us with capacities to receive the truth, at least in some measure. We need it for our guidance through life. It will be a strange thing if He does not offer it in such measure at least as we can receive. Philosophically a Divine revelation is the most natural thing in the world, provided that your philosophy is, in general, a spiritual philosophy.

In these days, though the main interest in religious study has been largely on the psychological rather than the Divine side, there is no great tendency to question the possibility of a Divine revelation; but there is a great tendency to question the possibility of one unique and universal revelation. There is a tendency to suppose that this supreme Spirit must of necessity manifest Himself in quite different forms to different people, showing different elements of His nature to different civilizations and so forth. And of course, there is a groundwork of truth in that contention. It is certainly true that the West and the East will tend, even if there be one revelation given, to apprehend most easily different elements within it, and also probably to ignore other elements that are really there. It may be that from one Divine act of revelation there may arise a number of quite different general theories about the nature of God simply because the human recipients of this revelation have attended to different elements in the gift put before them. This is true; but it is not a necessary consequence of this, that a single act of revelation, which may become the focussing point of all truth for all mankind, is out of the question. Nor is it true that there could not be a particular manifestation that is adequate to the universal truth, if you are thinking in terms of Spirit. If you think in terms of matter, it would be true; and a great deal of the confusion in our minds results from the fact that we have materialistic conceptions even in our handling of spiritual things.

One of the leading heresies of the present moment is the heresy that there is no such thing as matter, that it is an illusion. If you will study scientific researches into the nature of matter, I think you will be rather surprised by the complexity of the illusion which the human mind seems to have developed out of itself. That, however, while it is astonishing, would still be possible. But you notice this result in any of the thinkers who deny the existence of matter; a nemesis follows, in that they proceed to set up a materialistic conception of spirit, and leave themselves after all with what is really a materialistic universe. When you find such an argument as this: 'If God is Spirit and God is everywhere, there is no room for matter,' you know that the author had a purely materialistic conception of spirit. Spirit does not occupy space. You may have spirit everywhere and the whole universe open for material existence as well. There is no contradiction. Spirit does not manifest itself through the occupation of space, but in thinking and feeling, in loving and hating; and these things don't take up any room. You can have any number of stars in a universe in which people love one another.

We must begin by doing full justice to material existence, recognizing it as a part of the universe, and indeed as the groundwork of the universe, which exists for the sake of the superstructure as the foundations of every building do; and then we are free to go on with our inquiry into the nature of spirit with not nearly so much danger that the material elements in nature are going to obtrude themselves where they are genuinely out of place. This inquiry must be conducted in terms of quality, and not in the terms of quantity, which belong to matter. It is true that only a portion of any material substance could be manifested in a particular place or at a particular time. But that is not true of quality, which is the category appropriate to spirit. People sometimes say: 'How much of God was revealed in Christ? If you believe as a Christian that God was revealed in Christ, how much of Him was revealed?' Well, all of Him that is relevant: His love, and His holiness, which is part of His love, is all there. If the love that was in Christ was a perfect love for all men, there is nothing that can make it any greater, for it is already an infinite. You have reached a logical limit, seen to be a limit beyond which it is self-contradictory that you should ask to go; there cannot be more love than absolute self-giving to all.

Further, we get considerable help here, I think, from our experience in that sphere where man comes nearest to spiritual creation, short of the moral and religious life. That is in the sphere of art. In art a man is to an enormous extent master of his material. The greater the artist, the more master of it he is. And the whole object of art—an object sometimes, surely, achieved under the limited conditions in which every human artist must work—is to give a perfect individual embodiment of a universal truth or value. If a poem is a really good poem there is no way of telling anybody what it means, except by reading it to him. If he says 'I cannot see it,' you must read it to him again. You may give him hints to put him on the track; you may give him an analysis to show him the skeleton inside the living frame; but if you want him to know what the poet said you must read him the poet's words. Here, in the great phrase of Emerson, 'The word is one with that it tells of.' There is no other expression of the poet's meaning, though its range may be immense; there is no other expression of that whole meaning except this one concrete thing which, on its physical side, is a number of black marks on white paper. It is the same with other branches of art. In artistic activity, and in artistic appreciation we do, as a matter of fact, find particular cases which are adequate representations of the universal that lies behind them.

It is the same in moral conduct. The life of a great man is the real expression, not one possible alternative expression, but the one irreplaceable expression of the spirit, the general universal[1] spirit, which is his personality. This spirit is the principle that gathers them all together and gives them their meaning.

Further, it is worth mentioning (although it is only indirectly relevant to my point this morning, and we shall return to it in the last lecture)—you only get the meaning

---

[1] I don't mean, of course, 'universal' as related to the cosmos, but universal as related to all his particular actions at different times.

which gives value to all the parts when the whole is already present. If you think of any short poem you see at once that the meaning of it, the spirit of it, entirely determines each expression. It is a perfectly coherent and systematic whole; but you cannot deduce from the earlier parts what the later ones are going to be. It is not necessitated along the line of efficient causation where the antecedent determines the consequent. No one who has read the line, 'When I consider how my light is spent,' can deduce the remainder of the poem, or know that the poet a few lines later will say 'His state is kingly'. It is only when you get to the end, when you have grasped the whole of the poet's meaning, which determines with absolute precision the character and the place of all the parts, that you realize the necessity that each part should be what it is. The system of meaning fixes the nature or place of every word; but that system of meaning is only complete when the poem is finished. From this it follows that the true value of any occurrence may depend upon the future; the fact cannot be altered, but the value of the fact can be altered; and the real value of every fact is unknown until the course of history is complete.

Now we have to ask whether what has been said about the perfect embodiment of universal truth in a particular instance can be applied to the infinite spirit, to the spirit whose will is the ground of all existing things? Well, it all depends on whether you think the infinite Being has or has not a moral character. If the infinite Being is a mere undifferentiated substance, then I suggest, and even insist, that he fails to meet the demand for a self-explanatory principle. He is himself a mere brute fact. He is a block of being. If the ultimate reality is just substance without any quality or character—a mere stuff, as it were, which flowing into different moulds assumes different forms and characters, under the conditions of finite existence—it explains nothing whatever. It does not explain why the moulds are what they are, or why they succeed one another as they do. There can be no relation whatever between such a Being and human aspirations. He fails to explain both himself and the most important part of our experience. He is philosophically worthless.

But if the infinite Being has character, that character can be made known. Character always depends for its reality on its definiteness. When you speak of a 'man of character', you mean one the outlines of whose moral being are sharply cut, and on whom you can depend in all ways. It is the exact expression, for there is no real character in one whose spiritual state from moment to moment depends entirely on the accidental environment in which he finds himself. Such a being is merely reacting to external stimuli in the way that matter itself reacts; and it is in this lack of self-originated action that matter is most different from spirit. There is no difficulty in presuming that the infinite Being has character, if your analogy is not an indefinite substance, like a sort of clay which is to be moulded into a number of shapes, but is purpose and will.

It is true that a Being who has character is not logically infinite. If He is love, He is not hate; if He is righteous, He is not capricious: and so forth. But there is no logical ground for demanding as the explanation of the universe a Being who is logically infinite. Being in general is a possible object of contemplation, but it is the thinnest and emptiest of all concepts. What philosophy requires is a Being who is infinite in the sense that He depends on nothing other than Himself while all else depends on Him. Such a Being must be conceived (as we saw) in terms of Will. And Will is only real in the degree in which it is definite.

It still remains a great problem, the supreme religious problem, how a purpose and will such as can satisfy our moral aspirations can also be the ground of the universe in which we live. This is the problem of evil, which becomes all the greater in proportion as you insist on the character of the ultimate Being. It is only those people who have a vivid conception and conviction of the holiness of God who are sharply brought up against the problem of evil. You find it governing the Hebrew literature as it does no other ancient literature, because the Hebrews felt the contradiction between their experience and the Holy God to whom in their worship they had drawn near. You find it pretty strong in Plato, because he has a great conviction that only Good can explain things. It is hardly present in Aristotle, who has not that great conviction and whose doctrine of the ultimate source of being is simply arrived at by a line of physical argument—the necessity of a being who can set things in motion without itself being set in motion by anything else. It is in proportion as men believe in the character of the infinite Spirit that they are brought up against evil in the finite world. But to that problem we shall return a little later.

There is no sort of intellectual or philosophical difficulty in supposing that this universe is grounded in an infinite spiritual purpose and will; in fact, the preponderant weight of argument is decisively on that side. And if it be so, there is no difficulty in principle about the occurrence of one particular manifestation of that character in its perfect embodiment. But there are certain conditions that the manifestation has got to fulfil. It cannot take the form of an intellectual statement; it cannot be a doctrine; because such a doctrine would either be a very partial formula or else entirely surpass our capacity to apprehend. Just because the philosophical method cannot be adequately applied by the finite mind in a finite period, therefore nothing that is in the nature of a philosophical statement or disquisition could conceivably be the form in which the final and universal revelation is made. It is only possible in one way. It is possible in a life, which is the proper mode for any spiritual manifestation in this world.

What, then, becomes of the authority of church doctrines? It was never ultimate. When I say the creed, I say 'I believe in God'; but I don't say another creed about the creed—'I believe in the creed'. The creed itself is not an object of faith; and such authority as these formulations have is mainly the authority of a vast range of experience summed up in brief declarations. The aim of making such declarations was mainly negative, it was to declare that any theory which neglected or ruled out any part of this experience must be untrue. In fact, most of the formulated Christian doctrines were set down and defined in order to rule out certain tendencies of thought. There were those who thought that in the life for which Christians claim that it is a perfect manifestation of the infinite spirit, there was only a partial presence of Divinity; the Church sets down the phrase 'Perfect God'. There were those who in their insistence on the Divinity lost interest in the Humanity; the Church sets down the phrase 'Perfect Man'. It is not the concern of creeds to reconcile these things with one another. That is the task of theologians and of everybody interested in the intellectual study of the question. The concern of the Creeds is with the vitalizing experience on which the Church depends, and it sets down statement after statement to safeguard the fulness of that experience against those who would explain it away.

Anyone who wishes to throw overboard any of its formulations is incurring a very great responsibility. I am not one who would claim that the creeds are necessarily final. I do say the weight of authority behind them is so great that it is improbable that we shall find them wrong —supremely and enormously improbable. Further, I shall draw attention to the fact that they are not open to the attack commonly made upon them of consisting of Greek philosophy. If you will actually turn to one of those documents and read it, you will see that there is hardly any Greek philosophy in it at all. Nearly every article states either a fact of historical occurrence or else a spiritual experience. The statement that Christ was crucified under Pontius Pilate is not Greek philosophy. There is no Greek philosophy in the Apostles' Creed; and there is none in the 'Nicene' Creed except the phrase 'of one substance . . .' The emphasis of these documents is entirely concentrated upon the Life in which the revelation came.

As I have said, it is quite possible that other nations, other forms of civilization, will see in the Divine Revelation elements that we have not seen. They will therefore produce theologies different from ours. If they find it necessary to draw up formulations of faith different from our formulas, forewarning people against intellectual adventures which can only end in disaster, by all means let them do so. We shall ask them to keep in mind the results which come from our apprehension of the Divine act, and that they should not in formulating their apprehension come into conflict with what we have formulated as a result of ours. Let them have their own formulations; but they will be wise to take account of our experience and not throw it aside.

What we must desire is that, when all men have come together into the one allegiance of Jesus Christ, there shall be built up inside the Church as a whole such a complete understanding of Him as can never be possible to any isolated race or civilization. The West by itself can never know Christ in His fulness; nor can the East. It is only the Catholic Church holding them together that can do that. By holding together all the different types of religious life, experience, and aspiration, it will make available for all the treasure of a fuller knowledge than any man or any race by itself could reach, and will offer to each of us as individuals the fulness of that knowledge that we may live by it.

These documents, which we call creeds, are all concerned with the Life. I am going to consider to-morrow the question whether that Life itself so reveals God as to meet the philosophical requirements that I have tried to outline. I know perfectly well that anyone is at liberty to say—'Yes; no doubt you were careful to state the philosophical requirements in such a way as to be able to show us that your faith met them.' I don't deny it for an instant; but I also point out that I have certainly not deliberately falsified the statement of the philosophical claims with this object. What you have to consider is not my motive in presenting them as I do, but whether the presentation is true or false. If this is, as a matter of fact, the right way to approach the philosophical question of ultimate truth, then it does not matter that I had undoubtedly a strong personal interest in showing that the claims of philosophy are such that the Christian faith can meet them. Let us consider for one moment the characteristic nature of the Life, for which it is claimed that through it this full revelation can be and has been given.

The difficulties of the subject entirely arise from its being so familiar that we take it all for granted and never think about it, so that it is a very unaccustomed direction for most of our minds to take. For the main point which I have to urge upon you is that which I have already suggested, that in any life you do have the necessary, the unique, the irreplaceable expression of the spirit that dominates that life; and further, that in the degree in which that spirit is strong and pure it gives unity to the life, setting all its phases and all its actions in the right proportion; and above all this, that the exactness and the fulness of the expression entirely depend upon the particularity of the conduct. If you have a man who is full of religion and goodwill towards mankind, pursuing the even tenor of his way in a moderately comfortable existence in a small villa in the suburbs of a town, distributing his charity with genial good-nature and so forth, but otherwise living like anybody else, you get in such a form of life comparatively little opportunity of expression for the spirit which is the universal truth behind it, just because it is so like the lives of other people; just because it is so general, it fails to express the universal, not because there is a conflict between the general and the universal, but because there is conflict between expression and generality. Every artist knows that a universal only finds expression in what is perfectly individual. Indeed, individuality is the perfect synthesis of universal and particular, and if either fails the individuality is lessened. The more detailed you make the expression, the better expression it will be, provided the spirit expressed is always constant. If it is, then you will still have a unity of all the diverse detailed pieces of conduct. Consequently we shall not be surprised to find in that Life, for which the claim is made that it expresses the universal spirit, that it belongs to a particular time and a particular place, that it was lived under the conditions of a comparatively narrow circle of people, sharply marked off from all other, that it fully accepts these limitations and expresses itself in and through them. On the contrary, we shall rejoice in all that. It is only through such particularity that our Lord can give any detailed expression, which means real expression, of the universality of His Love. Love above all things requires such expression; because love must show itself in service to this one and that one under the conditions of their existence. It cannot be shown merely on the broad scale and in general terms. It must be individual. Therefore in the close relationship between our Lord's historical ministry and the conditions of His time the Christian will find no difficulty or perplexity at all; for what is important to him is not that the Lord did this particular thing or uttered this particular precept, but that in all of these you find one single spirit pervading the whole life, and that a spirit of such kind that it can find its operation everywhere in all times and in all places and through all persons of all races.

For there is one other requirement which a spiritual philosophy will make of any universal principle if it is to be accepted as the explanation of the world. What is it? It is that the spirit itself must be such as can operate plainly in all places. Now there are two great goals set before us by St John in his First Epistle which I have been taking as a sort of guiding star of our thought in these lectures, which you can always pursue with absolute perfection, though one of them with more thoroughness of success than the other, so that your devotion to them can always be complete and active. One is truth and one is love. You can always not only desire the truth, as you can always desire beauty, but you can always be actively promoting it as you cannot be always creating beauty; you can always be so directing your own mind that you are furthering the cause of truth in the world. Truth to all fact, and truth in all thought. But you may not always be able to attain to the truth you seek. Love is always supreme over the world in this sense at least—there is no conceivable situation in which it is not possible to show absolute perfection of love. I do not think there is any other quality of which that can be said. At least it is true of love; and the infinite spirit for whom it is claimed that He is the source of being and the explanation of the world must be at least this, whatever else besides—perfect and absolute love. Nothing else corresponds with this very obvious fact of universal experience. In one sense it is so obvious that one is almost ashamed to labour the point; but it is also overwhelmingly important that wherever you are you can practise and show love. Does not it tell you a good deal about this universe in which we live, that love is one of the things, possibly the only thing, that can never be excluded by circumstance?

3

CHRIST THE COMPLETE REVELATION

YESTERDAY we passed from the consideration of those methods of inquiry which deal with the state of the human mind in its religious activity to that method of inquiry which endeavours to establish, or estimate approximations to, ultimate truth; and we found that the one principle known to us, which is capable of satisfying the philosophical demands, is that which we call Spirit. The Spirit who meets this intellectual need must be One. It is clear that there is a totality of things. It is as the explanation of that totality conceived as such that we have needed to find some self-explanatory principle; and we found it in Spirit. As we proceeded we passed beyond what seems to be the farthest point to which the philosophical method can guide us, and came to what Christians claim to be the gift of God in a direct revelation made through a Divine act. So we were led, further, to conceive of this ultimate spirit in terms of love. And we found, in our concluding section, that this also fits in with one of the observable facts about the universe, namely that love is one of the things, perhaps the one thing, that can never be excluded by circumstance.

If this be so, then our conception of the unity of the world will not be one that excludes the very utmost variety and diversity; for love is always of individuals; a love that is merely a love of things in general or of the universe in its totality, apart from concern for individuals and apart from any desire for a love that shall be returned, is something quite different from any love that we know, and to call it by the name of love would be an abuse of language. If we conceive the unity of the world, not in the materialist terms of substance, but in the spiritual terms of love, then that unity will not be the unity of the absolutist philosophy in which all distinctions are at last merged, but it will be the unity rather of a family, of a comradeship where all the different members, with their characteristics unimpaired, are united by a common origin, or a common purpose, or a common affection. It is this unity that ought to be most manifest upon earth in the Church; it is the unity of which the supreme expression is that of the Blessed Trinity. Please remember that we are not as Christians called upon to go out into the world and persuade men that God is a Person. That would be persuading men to a heresy. When we speak of God in personal terms, as we are bound to do, we speak of Him as three Persons—the Person loving and loved in return, the Person loved and loving in return, and the personal relationship between these Persons. There are three Persons in the one God; and as Professor Webb, in his Gifford Lectures, has been telling us, what religion is concerned about is not to establish a single centre of consciousness in the Deity but to secure our faith that in the Godhead there is that which can support personal relationship with us, when we come into fellowship with

God. That is what matters for religion, and there is no need for that to tie down our conception of the Divine to the idea of an individual consciousness which is what we generally mean by Person.

With such a conception of the unity of the world we are not in any way belittling the independent spiritual life that has started upon its course in finite spirits. Nor can I for a moment believe that that finite life, once started, ultimately becomes re-absorbed again into the infinite upon which it depends. If that were its destiny I could see no use in its having ever begun. Why in the world should a transcendent unity differentiate itself, even in the realm of 'appearance', into all the multiplicity of our experience, if it is in the end to be—or in ultimate reality is all along—what it would be if the apparent multiplicity had never been? Such a process is meaningless and therefore philosophically to be condemned.

But the meaning of the finite life only begins to be discovered and its justification supplied when we think of the nature of God as Love, and of finite life, therefore, as the object of that love from which He seeks, in each individual, the characteristic answer, the typical response. You have a principle here which is capable of a limitless expansion, for there is no limit which can in the nature of things be set to the expansion of the volume of love; and the meaning of the world is seen to be that the volume of love uniting the finite spirits to God the Father of spirits, and to one another, should steadily increase and swell both in volume and intensity through the ages. There is at least no contradiction in such a notion, and it is in the centre of such a scheme that Christians set the figure of Christ. Our special subject to-day is to ask: 'Does the historic life of Christ meet these requirements?'

First let us look at it in its bearing upon human relationships. What would seem to be the most fundamental of all principles governing our Lord's ministry? I should say, without the smallest hesitation, Liberty. He absolutely refuses to take any steps that may bring Him adherents other than those who are drawn to Him through the motion of their own free will. Even His miracles He tries as a rule to conceal, because He knows that the sort of excitement that they evoke is not a kind to create really devoted, freely devoted, adherents. He does not appeal to them as evidence of His Divinity. On the contrary, with regard to the greatest of them all— the casting out of devils —he says: 'If I by Beelzebub cast out devils, by whom do your sons cast them out?' It is not on power that He rests His claim. John the Baptist, who as it would seem had once recognized Him, was puzzled in his prison by what he heard. He had thought of Him as the coming Messiah, the Son of God who should inaugurate the Kingdom of God on earth. In prison he heard of the works of the Christ, and what did they come to? A few blind men made to see, a few deaf men to hear, even a few dead people raised up, but no renovation of human society, no proclamation with irresistible power of the law of righteousness, no divinely appointed successor of David reigning from Jerusalem: none of these things—nor any manifestation such as the apocalyptic writers had led men to expect in the clouds of Heaven. So from the prison he sends to ask: 'Art thou He that should come or do we look for another?' and the answer is: 'Tell John again the things that ye do hear and see,' and, 'Blessed is he whosoever is not scandalized at me.'[1] Why? How is that an answer? Because it is not power that is the manifestation of the Kingdom of God—not power as men ordinarily conceive power—power, that is to say, that imposes upon men against their will. The Kingdom of God is the sovereignty of love. It desires none but willing adherents, and its method is never to impose allegiance upon men who do not want it. It seeks those who from their own free hearts offer their devotion.

It is the power of love only. For this reason our Lord begins with an absolute respect for the personality of all those finite spirits which are here the chief recipients of the Divine love. And all this culminates in the act of revelation from the Divine side. For what is the supreme and peculiar feature of Deity as revealed in Christ? Triumphant sacrifice. All the great thinkers of the world in one way or another came to the threshold of that thought; and there they stopped. They have all told us in one way or another that every finite thing fulfils its destiny so far as it plays its part in the scheme of the whole under the guidance of the supreme principle. So Plato, for example, sought for justice in the soul; he found it to expand into justice in the state, and he found that again expand into the Idea of Good in the universe; it is always the same principle, namely, that each departmental activity, that each psychological faculty or power, that each different class of citizens, that each different form of being, should do its own work, in its own position that it is qualified to fill, never claiming more and never giving less, according to the supreme principle of the universe which allots to each its place. We recog-

[1] It is a pity not to transliterate here.

nize that as broadly the sort of teaching that all philosophy gives. But what is the claim of that supreme principle upon you? Plato, with his great honesty, always shows his conviction, that in asking a man to be just, you are asking him really to give up something good. It would be better for his philosopher-king to contemplate eternal truth in selfish enjoyment of it than to go back and try to govern the state by his wisdom. But he must not do it, and Plato lays upon him the hard moral obligation to enter into practical life, saying that he will render his duty for we are laying a just demand upon just men. That is all. He cannot say it is good for him. On the contrary, if the philosopher has gained his wisdom not through, but despite, the civilization in which he lives, he will by no means seek to save society but will only seek to escape from the world without contamination. Plato sees no excellence in self-sacrifice. It may be a duty, but in itself it is an evil. The supreme principle has no claim upon men other than the claim of sheer stark duty. There is something wanting, something that the most aspiring minds had never dared to say: That just as the finite spirits are to live in service to the Supreme, the Supreme exists in service to the finite. That is the Cross.

The Cross is at the centre of Christianity not as an episode in history, but as the momentary manifestation of eternal truth. 'The Word was in the beginning with God' —the Word which was His utterance of Himself; for love can never be content to reside within itself; it is its very nature that it goes out and seeks expression; and so, because God is love eternal, there is the eternal utterance of God declaring His nature, so that it may be shared. That utterance is called His word. It is by the agency of the

Divine word, or as we may put it in other language, it is through the necessity that love is under to express itself, that there comes into being a universe both to manifest and to receive the love of God. And the whole of the created universe is, as the great Christian theologians have always said, implicit in the being of the Word. Then into that universe, which all the time is in some measure an expression of the Divine Love, there comes the full expression, in order to reveal to the world what had always been its own root principle, so that seeing it, the world might be won to a fuller and more complete response.

The life of Christ is a momentary manifestation of eternal truth; and it is good for us as a devotional exercise sometimes to read the Gospels, turning all the past tenses into the present, and to remember that what we read there is the expression, quite strictly, as I was saying yesterday, under all conditions of the time and place in which the expression occurred, of what is always true. And the culmination of this utterance is the Passion. The ultimate truth about God and His relation to the finite spirits is this, that 'when He is reviled He reviles not again, and when He suffers, He threatens not'.

Now that is the only possible mode of omnipotence in a world that contains free finite spirits. Once God had been pleased to create beings with hearts and souls capable of choosing for themselves—and therefore morally certain to choose for themselves in the special sense of choosing what they like for themselves—there was only one way by which He could still be omnipotent; it must be by revelation of His love in such a form as to win answering love. There can be no other. He could have controlled external events of course; He could have controlled our conduct, by sheer exercise of power; but then there would have been something that finally and for ever escaped His sovereignty— the heart and will of man, the highest thing He had made, the thing for which perhaps much of the rest was made. If that was to be won, it must be won in such a way that its allegiance was no contradiction of its freedom. Now it is a perfectly common experience that when we do things to please other people, our action is determined by what is their pleasure, and yet our freedom is never so complete. There is no act in which a man is so entirely self-determining as when he deliberately acts for the sake of another's pleasure or another's welfare. He does not in the least degree feel that he has been hypnotized or his will over-ridden, or that he is a mere passive instrument, reduced to a puppet by the other's will. On the contrary, he is then most of all himself; we know it perfectly well. There is all the difference in the world between acting in this way from love and acting under a kind of coercion that some powerful personality has put upon us without carrying our consent with him. If God is to become the determinant of our conduct in such a way as not to paralyse the will and heart that He has made, it must be by winning our love; and there is only one way, broadly speaking, in which our love is drawn out to those to whom it does not spontaneously go.

None of us in human shape are so entirely devoid of the capacity of love that we have no friends. But there is no supernatural merit in loving our friends; it is quite an easy thing to do; as Christ said, Do not the publicans the same? We do not require a Divine revelation in order to do that. The problem is to love our neighbour—the chance person with whom we are brought into contact by the accidents of life. There are some people who find it comparatively easy to love the Hottentots and the inhabitants of Timbuctoo—or at any rate to act as if they did—but fail entirely before the test of 'love thy neighbour', the vexatious family next door with their irritating habits and aggressive manners. That is always the test. Do you feel any natural sympathy, do you feel your hearts go out for the welfare of those with whom you are brought into casual intercourse, though they may be people of another race such as the Jew whom the Samaritan assisted, knowing that if his action ever came out, he would be cut by all his friends for all the rest of his life? That is the test, and before that test most of us fail quite hopelessly and all of us in some degree. We shall, as a matter of fact, only find the power to love other men in this way through first learning to love God. But there are some of those fellow-creatures of ours who show us how love may be drawn up from our hearts even though it did not spontaneously grow. These are those who show love to us, and there is no man who can be quite indifferent to the discovery that some one else cares for him enough to be put to serious inconvenience and trouble for him. It is not the trouble itself; it is the realization of the love expressed in it that moves us; and we are never quite indifferent.

Love always expresses itself in one way—sacrifice. For the essence of sacrifice (now that the word has been moralized by Christ) is the readiness to do or to suffer something which, apart from your love, you would not have chosen to do or to suffer. It need not necessarily be painful, though it often will be; but there is the essence of sacrifice the moment your will is altered by the consideration of another's happiness or welfare. Your will is then surrendered to their good. As it is thus that some men can draw out our affection, so it is that God must draw it out. Most of us are bound to admit that we are not in love with Love; and our care for love has to be drawn out of us by something that is done outside of us. At this point the human will is simply and utterly powerless. Our freedom does not extend to this point. My will—that is to say, my settled purpose in life—can control a great many of my impulses, and most of us ought to brace our wills up to far stricter control of our impulses than we are in fact practising; but what it cannot do is to give itself a new direction. We may, by having our eyes opened to the real nature of the thing that we are doing, be brought to dislike what hitherto we have liked; we may even of ourselves follow out some train of thought which shows to us the real result and implication into remorse, and through remorse into repentance, and through repentance into change of impulse. But beyond that you cannot go. If you are in fact in love with things that do not deserve to be loved, you can only be altered, not by an effort of your own, but by coming into contact with something which manifestly deserves much more love. You may call this the doctrine of original sin if you like; the fact is there. Mankind is not going to rise to the heights which alone correspond with God's purpose for it on the strength of its own resources. And that is what the doctrine of original sin really means. Something has got to be done to us and for us before we are capable of being what God desires that we should become.

God then, in order to be Omnipotent, and in order to fulfil His will concerning us and make us the thing that He desires us to be, was bound to manifest Himself in sacrifice. And that is the first significance of the Cross at the centre of the Christian faith. God manifested to the world what He is ready to bear at the hands of the world in order that the world might realize what sin and selfishness mean to Him; and so the first significance of the Cross is its power to create penitence. But if the Cross is thus the centre of the Christian revelation of God, for which we claim that it is an universal revelation, we must follow this thought further. There has been a great deal of difficulty, some of it quite unnecessary, introduced into Christian theology, largely by the application of legal terms which are not in place. There is a reality of judgment, most assuredly; Christ's presence in the world automatically effects a judgment; men are judged or classified as on the side of light or on the side of darkness by their reaction to the love of Christ. In this sense there is a constant operation of judgment, and the judgment works itself out in historical events, as I shall try to show tomorrow. But that common picture of the Great Assize is singularly misleading, for it begins and ends in a conception of the relationship of God and man which is infra-Christian. The prisoner in the dock does not generally feel himself called upon to suffer agonies of remorse by contemplating the distress of soul he is occasioning to the worthy man on the bench. His sole concern with the magistrate or the judge is to find what the man is going to do to him. In the Law Courts forgiveness means remission of a penalty. Forgiveness does not mean that between a child and his father. It

does not mean that between friends. If my friend feels outraged and separated from me by my conduct, and I want
to renew the friendship and come to say, 'Can you forgive
me?' I do not mean, 'I hope you are not going to prosecute,'
and I do not mean, 'I hope you are not going to use
the stick.' I mean 'Can you let us go on as before in spite
of it all?' That is what forgiveness means—the restoration
of the old intimacy in spite of the way in which it had been
forfeited by betrayal. That is what God's forgiveness is.
'We have not received the spirit of bondage, the spirit of
the slave, that we should relapse into fear, but we have
received the spirit of adoption whereby we cry Abba,
Father.' There is no phrase in the New Testament more
full of Christian experience than that. The whole significance of the relationship between master and slave is that
the slave is told what he has to do, not why he has to do
it. He is punished if he disobeys, and he may possibly be
rewarded if he carries out the task particularly well. But
that is the end of the relationship. And that is not the
relationship between the Christian and his Lord. 'I have
not called you servants, (or slaves), but friends, for the
servant knoweth not what his lord doeth, but whatsoever
I have heard of my Father I have made known unto you.'
We have been brought into the intimacy of God. We know
His purpose; we know His character. We are not merely
given commands to carry out, with penalties if we are dis-
obedient. We have not received the spirit of bondage or
slavery that we should fear, but the spirit of adoption—
(it is of His mercy that He took us to Himself)—whereby
we cry, in the word Christ used in the Garden, 'Abba'.
The fact that that Aramaic word fixed itself in the Greek of

the New Testament is a standing witness to the truth that the realization of the Fatherhood of God was something new and fresh to those who had learnt to draw near to God with Christ as their guide. It meant something new. It had been used before, but it was something new to those who heard Him saying to His Father, Abba. From such a Father the forgiveness we seek is the forgiveness which restores the old relationship. And He can offer that forgiveness because He has shown us what it costs Him. He is not an angry hostile Deity who needs to be propitiated.

But there is language about propitiation in our classical documents. Yes; for while it is true that God always desires our welfare and never desires that ill should befall us, and in that sense is never hostile to us, yet while our souls are sinful there is antagonism in the nature of God against us—something that may fitly and rightly be called the 'wrath of God', just as a father may rightly be in antagonism against the evil passions which for a moment dominate his child. No doubt it is true that God hates sin while He loves the sinner; only remember that sometimes our sin is not something accidental, put on like our clothes. Sometimes, and in nearly all of us in some respect, it is an essential characteristic of our nature as we now are. My will is not something other than myself; it is myself in action. If my will is set on the wrong things, then I am set on the wrong things. I am in opposition to God, and God for my own sake must be in opposition to me. And so there is propitiation in the sense that there is an alienation between God and man, a real antagonism of spiritual impulse, to be removed. And Christians believe that the antagonism in God against us is removed by the sufferings of Christ. How so? Well, if we read our New Testament carefully we shall not be in any doubt; it is not because the penalty due to us has been visited upon Him; that would make the Atonement flatly immoral. It is because the life of Christ, and above all the death of Christ, possesses transforming power.

The centre of St Paul's theology on the subject is the great phrase 'In Christ'; he will say that everything that is true of Christ is true of the Christian, because the Christian is *in* His Master. If Christ died the death penalty of sin, then so did we in Christ. We died in Christ; we are risen in Christ. Does that sound to us as at least exaggeration? No, because God sees in us the work Christ will one day have accomplished in us, and the antagonism ends, not because He is satisfied with the sufferings of another on our behalf, but because if we are in any degree united to Christ, if our hearts are in any degree open to Him, we shall be moving on from stage to stage in the process of transformation into His likeness till at last 'when He appears we shall be like Him because we shall see Him as He is'. And so in the hymn we say, 'Between our sins and their reward we set the passion of Thy Son Our Lord'— because we have first said, 'Look, Father, look on His anointed face, And only look on us as found in Him': not as we are—('our prayer so languid and our faith so dim')—but 'as found in Him', as we are in the light of the transformation that He is already accomplishing in us and will carry through to perfection unless we resolutely block the way. So all that language about the propitiatory aspect of the Cross must always be combined with the other great Christian doctrine that we are 'In Christ'—already in the sense that our hearts (we trust) are open to His influence, and prospectively in the conviction that that influence will at last transform us into His own likeness.

But once more is not this whole attitude of God to the evil of the world fundamentally immoral? Has God any right to restore us to the old relationship when once we have sinned at all? Here you come to another aspect of the necessity of the Cross as the centre of a religion which is also to be a philosophy. There is a moral danger in forgiveness. Human forgiveness is terribly often tainted with it, and we have all known lately during the war the real difficulty of forgiveness which shall be free from the charge that it makes light of evil and condones sin. We have known that those who have resisted the movement of the spirit of forgiveness in our country towards Germany, for example, have rested their case partly on the insistence that we must not overlook the atrocities that Germany committed. Well, there are many answers to that particular plea. It comes very near to setting up man in the place of God. It ignores certain actions committed by our own nation in various parts of the world, for which we also have to seek forgiveness. But when we come to this thought in relation to our conception of God, it is true that it would be bad for mankind to be assured that God forgives their sins, if that were all; because then mankind could say, 'After all, He does not much mind : it is all right.' It is not all right. The doctrine of the forgiveness of sin would be immoral if there were not a Cross. But no Christian is ever going to say, 'It is all right; God did not really mind'; for the Christian has heard the word of pardon from the lips of the Crucified, and no man who has knelt at the foot of the Cross to receive his pardon will go away and say, 'He did not mind.' He minded, and He minds now, with an intensity which can only be expressed in the fact that it gives Him the Agony and the Bloody Sweat, it gives Him three hours of anguish and that appalling sense of desolation when it seemed that the cause of God had failed, that God had failed Himself. That is what our sin means, and because He has manifested this He can receive us back to His heart without any danger of lowering our moral standard or weakening our moral fibre. On the contrary, to any man who really believes, evil assumes a terror that it never had before. There is a depth of meaning in that marvellous saying in the Psalms: 'There is mercy with Thee; therefore shalt Thou be feared.'

That, I venture to say, is the central point, the distinctive factor, in the Christian conception of God. It is that God wins His way in the world, not by over-riding, but by winning out of men's hearts a perfectly free allegiance, through the revelation of what their alienation from Him costs Him. That is the inner secret of the love of God. Is that a revelation which has any special significance for particular races, for particular times, particular civilizations? Plainly not. Plainly it is wholly independent of all those conditions. It goes right under all of them to those matters of the spiritual life in which all of us are perfectly at one. In the end of the day there are two poles and about one of them our life must centre: love which is God, and self. And the only question in the spiritual life in the last resort is whether our lives are set more in one direction or more in the other. At the moment no doubt most of us are hovering with a good deal of uncertainty between them.

The course of our life is more like an ellipse about the two poles than a circle about either of them. But it is probably being drawn nearer to one or the other of those poles. To become centred upon love of God, to care for the good things of the spirit, love and joy and peace, and all those excellencies by the possession of which we are united to other men, is salvation; and to become wholly centred upon self and to care for the good things, possession of which separates us from other people and excludes other people from a like possession, is damnation. These are the two goals possible to the human soul, and towards one or other we are moving. The whole 'scheme of salvation' is the process of transforming us out of selfishness into love. But there is nothing in that which belongs to Europe or to Western civilization that is not equally applicable to every human being. The way in which it is presented, the way in which the whole matter is set, may vary indefinitely. The elements which receive most emphasis will vary; sometimes it is the removal of the alienation between God and our will; sometimes our mystical incorporation in the person of Christ; sometimes the suffering in the heart of God which our sin causes Him, and by the revealing of which He is able without any demoralizing influence to receive us into perfect fellowship with Himself, however often we betray His trust. One or another of these may receive more emphasis under different conditions of human civilization, but the central conception of God giving Himself in love to the world and thereby uniting the world to Himself in free surrender of the finite will to the supreme Spirit which has so revealed itself—that is not particular in the sense of belonging to only one time or place; it belongs to the universal nature of spirit. And it is so that we claim that the revelation that was given once at a particular time in a particular place, in Palestine under Pontius Pilate, is a revelation to all men and to all places for ever.

The one thing we are bound to require, as it seems to me, is that men shall say that this Christ is very God, not for the sake of doing honour to Jesus of Nazareth—He did not claim honour for Himself—but because every thought of God which is not in accord with the character of Jesus Christ is idolatry, a false image of God; and the more we dwell upon it, the worse it will be for us. 'This is the true God and Eternal Life. My little children, keep yourself from idols.' These are perhaps the last words written in the New Testament, and they certainly sum it all up. We cannot ever have truce with the suggestion that Jesus of Nazareth was divinely inspired as others have been divinely inspired, and that God appears in certain aspects of His being in Him and in certain other aspects elsewhere; the moment that line is taken, you destroy conviction at the central point, namely that God is one Whose character we know, and know in perfect definiteness of outline, because it is the character of Jesus Christ. That is the Christian claim. We are, of course, very far from denying that men may learn abundantly from Christ without accepting the whole of that claim; and we are only too glad that they should do so. His treasures are for all mankind, and that all men should enter into them as they may and will must be a matter of happiness to His disciples. But nothing else than this is acceptance of the Christian religion. This is the Christian faith. This, we believe, is the power that can save the world.

4

DOES CHRISTIANITY WORK?

THE words with which I closed yesterday were that to faith in Christ we look for the salvation of the world. Do we look in vain? Does Christianity work? That is not only a practical question; it is fully in place in the consideration of the intellectual setting of our faith. For Christianity claims to be a religion of power, and if in fact it does not work, unless we can find the sources of the weaknesses that have beset the Church and also the way to cure these weaknesses, then the practical failure is a demonstration of the falsity of the doctrine. There is no other religion in which practical failure would be so fatal to the claims of theoretical truth.

We have claimed that the Almighty God is revealed in Christ, and to that end that Christ Himself must be the Almighty God. What can be the meaning of that in the world we know? The urgency of this problem is intensified, I think, by the modern, but I am sure also the true, way in which most people today approach the question. Most of the earlier theologians could be content to say that God took upon Himself human nature and lived in the world under the form of human nature, but that in the Incarnate there was no human Person; according to their doctrine the

Person is God only, His divine nature being associated with human nature.

We have come to know a good deal more about human nature than the earlier theologians did, and that mainly through Christianity itself. We have discovered in a very large measure something which was very vaguely apprehended by the older thinkers, namely Personality. It is a significant fact—perhaps you can lay a little too much stress upon it—but it is at least a significant fact that there is no word for personality in Latin, and no word for it in Greek. The word was coined to represent an idea which came into increasing prominence through men's knowledge of God and their resultant knowledge of Man. And as we study human nature, most of us at any rate have come to the conclusion that human nature, which is not fully individual, is not perfect human nature; therefore if our Lord was truly Man, then He was also *a* man. I daresay in this audience it is hardly worth-while to insist on that point of view, because, according to my experience, most of the people in our universities feel quite sure that He was *a* man. The question they are asking is whether He was also God, and in what sense He is inclusively Man. Remember, the old Church was altogether convinced He was Man, and very nearly unanimously convinced that He was not *a* man at all. He was the person of God living through human nature, but not a human person; that was the main trend of the older theology. Yet, as I say, I am quite sure that this newer claim that we must see in Him a human individual as well as the Divine Person is a sound claim, and you will rightly say to me—'How are the two to be connected?' So I must pause in the general process of my argument to deal with this question, although it must be in short space.

First I will say this: supposing Christianity is true; supposing that our Lord is indeed a man and also God, you must not expect—it is monstrously unreasonable to expect —a complete detailed psychology of His Person. That a man who is not God should offer a psychological account of a man who is also God would be monstrously presumptuous. We cannot expect to grasp that mystery and analyse it as we can analyse, to some extent, our own states of consciousness. If the doctrine is true, it will baffle our minds at least until we also are perfectly united with Christ and in Him with God. And therefore we are not to expect that we shall find the kind of demonstration which makes everything seem neat and tidy; but we have the right to expect to find certain clues, various strands connecting up what must remain to us two aspects of our Lord's person, the human and the divine, in such a way that, as we follow up these clues, we obtain a progressive understanding, never complete, but always deeper and deeper, of that supreme mystery.

Now if we are to claim for our Lord that He is really ruler of the world, we are bound, I think, in some shape or form to assent to that doctrine that we were glancing at yesterday of His inclusive personality. The root of it is the Christian's experience expressed by St Paul in the words 'In Christ'. The Christian feels himself to be taken up into the personality of Christ, possessed by His Spirit, but yet not, as we saw, in such a way as to abrogate or annihilate the freedom of his own will. This bond-service is perfect freedom; and from that Christian thinkers have generalized, and have said that in Christ we see the human race collectively represented in one essential symbol, by which I mean a symbol which is itself a perfect instance of the thing it symbolizes. We have, therefore, two sides always to consider, and the two sides are both in the New Testament. Sometimes St Paul speaks of Christ as being Himself the whole Church; the Church is His body. But at other times, He is the head, and other members are necessary to the fulness of the body. So here Christ is the human race, corporately and prospectively. In Him we see what it is the purpose of God to accomplish in all men, and what God through Him and by means of Him is accomplishing; and in Him also we see individually the first fruits of humanity. He is the one man, chosen out from many sons of men, to be a perfect representative of humanity before God, and so far He stands as an individual apart from us in the individuality of His perfect human nature. But He is also that in which we see what we are to become, and therefore He seems to be in Himself all mankind. How can we understand this better?

First let us recall what was said in the second lecture, that any expression of a great truth depends for its power on the expression being perfectly individual. You know that, as soon as you consider any dramatic figure. Othello is a great expression of human jealousy, because he is a very individual jealous man. But if the dramatist merely stages an abstraction, who has no individual characteristics at all and merely acts according to the type for which he stands, then you get no real expression; you get only an allegory, and no dramatic experience. It is only by individualizing that you can get expression; and that is as true of universal truth as it is of any particular truth. The love of God, if it is to be fully expressed, must be expressed in individual form. That individual form we find in the individuality of Jesus Christ, which has been set forth before us once for all by the evangelists, particularly the Synoptic Evangelists. The Humanity there set forth is undoubtedly individual. We are reading of *a* human person. But that human person is so completely surrendered to God that in sober truth the Person of Jesus Christ is God; and only because this is so can He claim the allegiance of all men and so become inclusively Man.

We pass on to the consideration that what we find in the spiritual life is not something wholly alien from what we find in the normal life, but is the ordinary natural power transformed through its being raised to an altogether fresh intensity; and that is what we should expect if the position claimed in the first two lectures is true, namely that the whole universe is itself in its degree an expression of the mind and character of the God Who is fully revealed in Christ. Nature is not something alien from Christ. It is the lower stages of the process which finds the expression of its fundamental principle in Him. Let me illustrate this continuity of the natural and the spiritual. There is the fact of influence, and there is the undoubted fact that we are capable of concentrating our influence. If a number of people get together and resolutely direct their will-power upon some object that they have at heart, for example the sustaining of some one engaged in a great enterprise, there is no doubt whatever they send forth power to sustain him. There can be little doubt either that collections of people—or for the matter of that also individual persons—

but mainly collections, possessed by feelings of hatred and antagonism, damage those against whom their hatred is directed. That is the basis of the possibility of intercession. But in intercession you bring in a new factor. You don't direct your will immediately upon its object, but you direct it there through the universal knowledge and love of God, and you are not only releasing powers in God, which He is able to set in motion in answer to faith—(because it would have been bad for us if He set them in motion if there had been no faith, in as much as that would have stimulated our self-reliance and so have done us harm)— but also you are sending your own energy to be united with His loving care and directed by His loving knowledge into channels truer and more effective than your own limited love and wisdom could have suggested.

What intercession rests upon is the potency of concentrated influence. But you can go farther than that. Every great personality exercises an influence upon those round about him and upon posterity. As men come to understand, there leaps out from their own souls answering power, in the shape of some capacity to enter into the achievements, or at least the endeavours, of the great personality. That is the natural form, or the embryonic form in our limited experience, of what in the working of God is called the Holy Ghost. God had always been at work in the world, but only when He had revealed Himself in such a fashion that men could understand, so that their hearts went out in answer, could He release within their souls that Divine capacity which is implanted in men because they are God's children; only therefore when He had revealed His love was it possible for Him to exercise the fulness of His power over their lives. It is that fulness of Divine power over the lives of men which is specifically called the Holy Spirit, who therefore is said, quite rightly, to 'sanctify all the elect people of God'—that is to say, those who are chosen out among mankind to receive that greatest of all treasures, the fullest knowledge of God. It can only be so. That quality of human obedience and therefore that quality of divine control are only possible on those terms. Therefore, as St John says with absolute cogency, 'There was not yet spirit because Jesus was not yet glorified.' The completion of the revelation of the love of God in Christ's Life and Death and Resurrection and Ascension must come before this power of God can operate on the human soul, because the power consists in the particular kind of response which is made to love that is shown. This Holy Spirit of God coming thus through Christ *is* the Spirit of our Lord, *is* God in Christ in action amongst us, calling forth the divine power that is Himself out of our souls, so that as God commands from Heaven and as God pleads from Calvary, God out of our souls makes answer.

It is thus that the individual personality of Christ becomes all-embracing, just as a great leader of men may be said to carry them in himself and his will governs their action, not by hypnotism but by their voluntary allegiance to him. So in this case the same principle is carried to the utmost possible limit; because His love, as shown, is infinite, therefore there can be no barriers set to its all-embracingness. Christ, the individual man, necessarily becomes the all-embracing personality, because through Him all-embracing love is made known.

We have lately become familiar with the psychology of

crowd-consciousness. We do not as yet know very much about it, but we know enough to be aware that we are on the threshold of immensely important discoveries concerning human nature and the laws of its development; and we know broadly that the moral level of crowd-consciousness is always higher or lower than the average of the individuals composing the crowd. If the crowd is met together in the pursuit of an ideal end, then in the crowd there will be greater forces of idealism than in the average of the members composing it, taken separately; and quite equally, if it is met together for a selfish end or in hatred and antagonism, those spirits will be more potent than they are with the average members of the crowd. This is the basis of the Church. The Church is a corporate personality. It exists to be a centre of crowd-consciousness. But here the crowd-consciousness is not only something more idealistic than the average members who make up the Church; it is the person of Christ Himself. Because two or three are gathered together in His Name, He is in the midst of them and they become members of His body. The Spirit which works through them is the same spirit which perfectly worked through the individual man Jesus of Nazareth. He is not only *a* man, but also Man; but in order of time He is *a* man first. By virtue of the power of love and the operation of the principles of corporate consciousness working through the society of His disciples He becomes increasingly all-inclusive—Man; and only so is He quite perfectly representative of the divine purpose.

So St Paul saw it. In the Church all the old divisions had vanished; allegiance to Christ over-rode them. 'There is neither Jew nor Greek; there is neither bond nor free:

there is neither male nor female; for ye are all one man in Christ Jesus.' All the old divisions had become negligible. There was one man; and that man was Christ Jesus. If the will of Christ prevails throughout a society, for all practical purposes Christ is the only person there. So Christ is the Person of the Church as God is the Person of Jesus Christ.

St Paul goes on to say that at present this body of Christ is imperfect. It needs to be built up into its fulness; and we need to bring all men into the allegiance of Christ until we come to a perfect man—(not each of us separately become a perfect man; that is an entirely dull conception) —but until we all together make up the 'one man in Christ Jesus' grown to full stature, 'the measure of the stature of the completeness of the Christ.'

Then we turn back to the actual world. We have got a clue now. Even if we do not see the whole claim of Christianity at work, we see how it might come to work. So we turn back to our chief task in this conference, the comparison of Christ's standards with the world's practices, and the question of what we are going to do about it. Here let me enter a caveat. 'Christian ethics' is a purely historic term. A thing does not become right by being Christian, Rather it becomes Christian by being right. It is historically true that we discover a great many moral principles through Christ, but the righteousness of them and the obligation to obey them does not depend upon the authority from which they came. A thing is not right because God commands it; God commands it because it is right, and it is possible that the divinely inspired—or rather, to avoid a question-begging term—the aspiring conscience of a man, who does not at all accept the divinity of Christ, may independently be brought to the acceptance of principles which we have learned from Christ. Their rightness or wrongness depends upon themselves. What we come to Christ for is chiefly the power to live as He teaches; that is why our question—Does Christianity work? is so crucial.

The problem has two main limbs. First, the world, as we look at it, does not seem to reveal a God of Love. If we leave the Incarnation out for a moment and look at the rest of creation, it does not look as if Almighty Love had made and sustained it. That of course led in the early Church to the Marcionite heresy that the Creator of the world, the God of the Old Testament, was an inferior and even rather an evil Deity; and that the God of the New Testament as revealed in Jesus Christ was some one quite different. Mr H. G. Wells has lately revived this heresy.

That is one limb of the problem; and the other—to us more serious—is that so many who are not Christians in doctrine are much more Christlike in life than some of those who are Christians.

But the world does reveal the supremacy of love, first even in the bare struggle for existence in the evolutionary process. There you see quite clearly this principle: that the chief means by which a species succeeds, even in the competitive struggle, is by being co-operative. It is as the individuals hold together, and as individual interests are postponed to that of the species, that success is achieved. Co-operation is supreme over mere competition even at that level, and even in the purely competitive struggle. That is something already. When we turn to human civilization we see the revelation of the supremacy of love in the judgment of God at work in history. Think what it means to say that love is supreme over the world. To say that God is Love means, amongst other things, that every purpose or policy which is hostile to love, which rests on selfishness, is bound to end in disaster, for it is opposing the supreme principle of existence; and that every purpose or policy which is akin to love is bound to succeed, through whatever sacrifices it may first pass, because it is fighting in alliance with the supreme power. And in fact, at least in some measure, this judgment is apparent. Our Lord was careful to connect up His great sayings about His own coming in Judgment with the fall of Jerusalem—so much so that it is often difficult to know to which of the two He is referring. That is because they are not altogether two, but partly one. Jerusalem fell because of those qualities in it which led to the rejection of Christ, not through an angry God intervening to vindicate His outraged honour, but because this race, called to spiritual service, preferred secular ambition; that secular ambition made it a nuisance to Imperial Rome; Imperial Rome was not tolerant of nuisances; it was wiped out. Our Lord saw what was bound to happen. But when Jerusalem fell from that quality which led it to reject the Lord, the Son of Man came in His power. The authority of Law is vindicated when it operates against them who have broken it. But from the law of man there is escape; from the law of God there is none. And as you go down the great historic catastrophes you see that civilizations fell because they were based on principles other than those of Christ. Rome fell mainly because its whole strength was sapped by the institution of slavery and the handing over to slaves of one after another of the activities that properly belonged to citizens. Mediaeval Europe broke up because its Church had been false to the standards of religion, and fell back to gross worldliness. The French Revolution came because the old regime denied the rights of personality which were primary in the Christian conception of man. And we have seen a mighty nation, which declared that its welfare was its sole objective, also reduced to great desolation. In every one of these instances the Son of Man came in His power.

This judgment of Christ goes all the way down history. That is not cruel, because the aim that God has for us is not first our happiness, but first that we should become filled with that love which is the deepest thing in His nature and the best thing in the universe. And so the Incarnate Love, on the very threshold of His complete revelation of love, says of Himself: 'This is the stone which the builders rejected and is become the head of the corner; whosoever shall fall on this stone shall be broken, but on whomsoever it shall fall, it will scatter him like dust.' It is a fearful thing to fall into the hands of the living Love.

What love demands from us and seeks from us is not that we should be comfortable, but that we should be loving. It is quite true that the joy which comes with love is deeper joy than any other which can be found. It is quite true that even the supreme sacrifice was offered because of the joy which lay before Him, the redemption of the world from selfishness into love. But if you are thinking about happiness you will never find it; and so our Lord never said anything even remotely like this: 'If any man will come after Me I will deliver him from the pains of Hell, and give him the joys of Heaven'; but 'if any man would come after Me let him deny himself'—(let him say he is not there: it is a terrific paradox)—'and take up his cross'—put the rope round his neck. That is the quality of the demand, because the quality of love that is asked of us is a love completely dedicated. And because love is the best thing in the world, it is relentlessly stern against all self-seeking. Those who are self-centred will often feel the sternness of God before they can draw near to His tenderness. That truth stands out in the Gospel. The failure of the Pharisees is their self-complacent hardness and rigidity; and against that hard self-satisfaction there is launched the most terrific denunciation that you will find in literature—all the more terrible because there is no trace in it of personal spite, but a stark antagonism against the whole psychosis, which must be crushed before it can be renewed under the power of love. In such sternness, as in the judgments of God in history, you do see the supremacy of Christ so far. Of course, it is true that the purpose of a law is never to send people to prison for breaking it, but to prevent them from doing the things for which they might be committed to prison. And that, of course, the law by itself never can do. There are those against whom it is necessary to use this kind of force, spiritual if not physical; but that is purely preparatory in order that when humility has been attained love may make its appeal in its own natural form of service and sacrifice, and so the true life be called forth.

We turn to the second question. Is it true that Christians are not better than other people? Of course it is true that there are some non-Christians who are better than some Christians. The trouble begins so soon as the Church can take its great central truths for granted. That happened in the Middle Ages; the central truths became commonplaces and therefore lost grip upon the imagination. Men came to concern themselves about secondary matters, almost to the exclusion of the primary, and the Church itself became self-satisfied and worldly. And we are not out of that yet. It was Spinoza who bitterly asked why Christians differed from others not in love or joy or peace, or in any of the fruits of the Spirit, but only in the opinions which they held. But over against this it is true that there is a life in the Church which is without parallel on the face of the globe, a life which perpetually breaks out again and again when men suppose it is all over and done with. The Agnostics of England in the 'sixties and 'seventies had a phrase they were fond of using: 'We do not propose to refute Christianity: we shall explain it.' They regarded it already as a back-number for all intellectual purposes. They would explain how this delusion arose. It was not worth while to demonstrate where or how its doctrines were fallacious. No one would speak like that now. The Church is again a great force, and is a great deal more powerful now than in the eighteenth or first half of the nineteenth century. There may be more people standing aloof from it because it is less tolerant of indifference and apathy in its members, but there is a far greater volume of life inside it. We have been witnessing a great religious revival which has been spreading from the time when John Wesley swept into the arid controversies of the eighteenth century like the wind on the hill-tops, through the time when the Oxford Movement began building up a fresh conception of the corporate life, and liberal theology emphasized afresh the claim of intellectual truth, till now in our own day there is a coming together of different parts of the Church with all their different experiences of the treasures of Christ. There is life in the Church; and if you will look at it in history and not only compare our present practice with the ideal we have before us, though we must always be doing that, you will not have any doubt that there is a power of the love of God at work in the world through the Church. It is true that Christ expands Himself into this corporate person of the Church, and will at last build up a humanity which He can present to the Father with Himself, so that God may be all in all.

In the earlier lectures I tried to show ground for thinking that the universe is a spiritual system, but of course it is true that the resources of the spirit are not exhausted in the universe as we know it. That construction which I offered you, and which I wish you to consider upon its own merits and not because it is a convenient introduction to what follows, prepares the way for the reception of the belief that as we have one creation built up stage by stage through the evolutionary processes, every stage finding its own meaning only when the next comes upon it and completes and crowns it, so there are resources in the spiritual region of the universe that are by no means exhausted; and that the Holy Spirit of God which is at work all through the process is made perfectly manifest in Christ and by that perfect manifestation secures the fulness of His power over human lives. For there is one God; and if Jesus Christ is the express image of the person of the Father, so He is the perfect portrait of the Holy Ghost, and when we want to know who is this Holy Spirit that prompts us in our own souls, we shall read the Gospels just as we do when we seek to find out who is the world's Creator.

I think it is a coherent scheme which I have presented to you. I think it all holds together and makes up one consistent whole more capable of reconciling in one system all the facts of experience than any other that I have come across. But it is not proved. It is offered as a hypothesis. That is to say, it is a matter of faith; and faith is not knowledge. Faith means that we take this thing on trust and mean to live by it and see whether it vindicates itself in practical working. All faith is experiment; and you cannot have the result of an experiment unless you make the experiment. What we are now needing primarily is just courage—courage to put the thing to a practical test. It needs no courage, of course, to say to people that the creator of the physical universe, the animal world and our own bodies, is somebody who is revealed in our Lord. There are theoretical difficulties about it, some of which I have tried to indicate and have shown how I would begin to meet them. That does not want courage. What requires courage is to live in actual practice on the hypothesis that love is the supreme power in the world, and that success or failure depends on the harmony of our wills with love. There is no loss of freedom in such a belief. If you come to the edge of a cliff, it depends on yourself whether you will jump over or not. But when once you have jumped over, it no longer depends upon you whether you will go to the bottom or not. No one feels, however, that he is under any constraint because of the inexorableness of the law of gravitation; his will remains free, but he has this useful information about the universe by which to direct his choice. And incidentally it is worth while to point out that we cannot choose at all unless we can with practical certainty count on the consequences of our action. It is only the normal fixity of natural law which makes possible any valuable freedom of choice. And the relation of the law to freedom is the same in the spiritual world. If it is true that God is Love, then in every choice we make we are standing on the edge of a precipice. You can, if you like, make a selfish choice; and if you do you will be dashed to pieces sooner or later, and you will take others to destruction with you. That destruction may not be the last word. God may always, even to the end, have resources still in His Almighty Love by which He will call back all souls at last to Himself and save them from the results of their self-will and from that self-will itself. But in any calculable period of time you will, by your selfish choice, have involved yourself in loss, perhaps in ruin. There is no imposition upon your will; and what Love seeks is not a number of automata working as the wires are pulled, but a free response which need not be given, and whose value consists in the fact that you need not give it.

Because so many men do choose to do the selfish thing, the world is still apparently hostile to Love, and we see the supremacy of Love still very largely through its judgments on the selfishness of men as they overtake the world, and in the calamities that men bring upon themselves—not, allow me to say once more, by the angry intervention of a Deity whose honour is outraged, but by the steady operation of those laws by which He made the universe and which we can know, at least in the sense in which faith gives us knowledge.

Here is the view of things which is, I think, intellectually most probable. But faith rests not upon estimates of intellectual probability, but primarily on an appreciation of moral values. The man of faith is a man who says: 'I cannot prove that the world is like that, but it would be so splendid if the world were like that, that I will live accordingly. If I have made a mistake then I shall have died for a noble project. If I have not made a mistake, then I have done something for the greatest end that could be set before men.' That is faith. It is not yet quite religious faith, because a religious man believes that he knows who has set this supreme end before men, and that with this Author of his faith he is in fellowship. He is one who says: 'Though I cannot communicate this to another, yet I have the absolute certainty of the fellowship of Him in whom my trust is put. He has endured; He is enduring; and always through His endurance He brings about the victory which is the winning of free spirits to Himself. The world belongs to Love.'

CHRIST'S REVELATION
OF GOD
1925

5

WHAT OUR LORD PRESUPPOSED

CHRISTIANITY claims to be the truth. This is what supplies the basis of all its converting or missionary work. If it were, as some people suppose it to be, just a sort of drug appropriate to certain spiritual diseases, it would never be right to try to convert anyone until his spiritual condition had been diagnosed by an expert. Some such notion seems to be implied by those who say that we ought not to disturb the Africans, or the Indians, or the Chinese, but should leave them to the religion that suits them. Christianity is indeed the medicine for the ills of the world. But it derives its healing power from its truth. The Gospel nowhere shows a trace of interest in the psychological analysis of certain states of mind for which, when ascertained, it can prescribe a remedy. It consists of a proclamation which is either true or false; if it is true, the health of human life depends upon conformity to it; if it is false, its claim to provide guidance falls to the ground. The appropriate question is not, Does Christianity suit us? or the Africans? or the Indians? or the Chinese? The appropriate question is, Do we, or the Africans, or the Indians, or the Chinese, suit Christianity? The question is not, What are you going to do with Christ? The question is, What is Christ going to do with you?

This point cannot be over-emphasized. The Gospel does not begin with man's various needs and then offer ways of meeting them. The Gospel begins with God's truth, and calls upon men to live by it. A great deal of recent thinking about religion follows the other course. There is no harm in that, provided we do not force the Gospel into our mould. The philosophy of religion and the comparative science of religions are bound to start from the human end, for they must not make the assumption that the Gospel is the truth. If they reach that view at all, it will be at a late stage in their proceedings, after much evidence has been reviewed. But the Christian is one who, on whatever grounds, has accepted the Gospel, and, so far as he thinks about it, is engaged in working out what is involved in that assumption.

In my own view, that is the way in which, at the present development of our knowledge, Christian theology is bound to work. I do not believe that it is possible to arrive by cogent reasoning at the fundamental truths of Christianity. But if we make the hypothesis that they are indeed truths, we can, as I believe, vindicate that hypothesis by the rational completeness of the system in which it issues. This is a perfectly legitimate course to take, and is as scientific as any other, provided that we recognize what we are doing and avoid deceiving ourselves into regarding as intellectually certain what is still for us an unverified assumption. Faith, as I think, precedes its own rational vindication, not only as a matter of usual experience, but as a matter of inherent necessity. But that does not mean that it is itself irrational; it only means that it is itself the illumination whereby its rational grounds are discovered.

All of this is more relevant to our immediate purpose than may at first sight appear. For it carries with it two implications which we must keep steadily in mind. The first is, that if the Gospel is what it claims to be, we read it rightly only if we have our minds fixed all the while on God, and think of human relationships as consequential on the character and purpose of God. It is true that the Gospel lays an emphasis which cannot be exaggerated on those human relationships. No other religious system carries the whole force of religious feeling into this realm so completely as Christianity. But the second great Commandment, 'Thou shalt love thy neighbour as thyself,' is unalterably second, being a consequence of the first and not a possible substitute for it.

You have a graphic illustration of what I conceive to be the wrong way of treating the Gospels in Ruskin's book, *Unto this Last*. Ruskin has caused many readers of the Parable of the Labourers in the Vineyard to regard it as an illustration of how wages ought to be paid. I am sure this is completely wrong-headed. Whether or not wages ought to be paid solely according to need irrespective of desert or of the economic value of the labour remunerated, I am perfectly sure that this has nothing whatever to do with what our Lord then meant to impress upon His hearers. What that was, I shall describe in the next lecture; but it was an aspect of the relationship between God and man, not of the relationship between one man and another.

The first implication, then, of the belief that the Gospel is offered as a revelation of the truth, not primarily as a remedy for certain ills, is that it is to be studied by minds directed towards God. It is directly concerned to answer the questions: Who and what is God? What does He require of us? How does He enable us to meet His own requirements? It is only indirectly concerned with the questions: What have men discovered to be their chief needs? How does God's provision satisfy these? In this order of emphasis the New Testament is in true continuity with the Old, and I shall have in a moment to consider the validity of its method.

The second implication is that inasmuch as it claims to be truth, the Gospel must supply the clue to the whole of life and of reality. This claim forbids us to take it by itself and see how far it avails us, being content if it turns out to fit in with certain aspects of experience. But it is plain that the recorded life and teaching of Jesus of Nazareth does not supply in isolation, a complete philosophy. His teaching is markedly not systematic and deliberately avoids such completeness as would make it possible to treat it as a code of rules offered as a substitute for the Pharisaic code. He never teaches the existence of God; He takes that for granted, and assumes that His hearers will know what He means by the Name of God when He utters it. Plainly, then, He does not begin at the beginning. Those who come to learn from Him are assumed to have received and to have accepted much teaching about God already. What He does is to supply a new centre or focus of illumination, in the light of which all their former knowledge is not abolished but transformed. And this corresponds with what the whole position of the Gospel must be in relation to the total range of human knowledge and experience, if it is to make good its claim to be the truth. It is not in itself the whole system of truth, for it is not a system at all; it is a proclamation, a disclosure. But it is a centre or focus of illumination in the light of which all other knowledge is not abolished but transformed.

It is with such general notions in mind that I would approach our consideration of 'Christ's Revelation of God'. And they particularly concern our consideration of the first question, 'What did our Lord presuppose?' For, as we have seen, He did not come to write a new doctrine on the blank and empty tablets of minds till then without any religious convictions. He assumed a great body of conviction as already established. He did not come to give the first news about God; He came to reveal fully a God already revealed in part.

In quite general terms it is easy to answer our question. What our Lord presupposed was the Old Testament. There is no evidence of allusion to or interest in any other previous religious development. There was much in the higher philosophy of ancient Greece of which He could have made use; there was much in the religious traditions of Persia and India. To any of these there is no trace of a reference. But He assumes in His hearers not only acquaintance with, but acceptance of, the Old Testament; more than that, He appeals to it as an undeniable authority not only in controversy with opponents, but still more significantly in directing the purposes of His own life.[1]

If then we are to have a clear conception of what our Lord presupposed, we must gain it by forming as full and accurate an impression as we can of the doctrine of God

[1] Luke 4. 1–12; Matt. 4. 1–10.

conveyed by the Old Testament. We need not for this purpose go into any questions of criticism, for all of these are
irrelevant to the impression made by the Old Testament
upon the minds of the quite uncritical folk from among
whom the Lord chose His Apostles. But we must none the
less bear in mind the fact that its impression upon them
would be by no means the same as its impression upon an
uncritical English reader in our own day. To the uncritical
Englishman it is a single book, and its total impression is the
average impression of all its parts. But the Jews of the first
century were heirs of the tradition of which the books of
the Old Testament are the record. To them inevitably,
though very likely not consciously, it was a living thing,
and, because living, also growing.

This is a point of considerable importance. Citizens of a
country which has a long history of growth and progress
are actually moulded in their outlook by that history. Their
own minds are its fruit. Consequently when they read it,
they do so with minds which, however unconsciously, represent the growth and as a result take it for granted. People
of another country, or another civilization, read the same
history with different unconscious presuppositions. Thus
if I read the history of China, I read it from a point
of view external to it; my judgment on it is formed by
English, not by Chinese history. But when I read English
history I do it with a mind which English history has
moulded, so that my judgments upon it are in a sense part
of it, for they are the judgments formed by the present
phase of English history upon the process by which that
phase has been reached. Now this is parallel to the position
of a Jew of the first century in relation to the Old Testa-

ment. He was reading the history of which he was a product. But because he was a product he read it all in the light of its result. He could not help himself. He was that result, and must read the history in its light or else have no light by which to read it at all.

This brings us to a very important result. *The Apostles were not Biblical critics; but they read the Old Testament in a way that is only made possible for men of other races by Biblical criticism.* That is necessarily true of all men who read the history of their own nation. You read the history of your own nation as a development towards its latest phase, because you are yourself that latest phase. You read the history of another nation as a series of connected facts, but not necessarily as a development, unless and until you have acquired the historic point of view. The Apostles no doubt shared the prevalent belief that the Mosaic Law was the most sacred and most inspired portion of the Old Testament; but inevitably they read it through the eyes of the Second Isaiah, though they had no notion of his existence. Thus our inquiry into what our Lord presupposed does not involve us in any particular questions handled by critics; but it must involve us in acceptance of the general results of Biblical criticism; for the essence of this is that it regards the Bible as a growing thing and tries to trace out the course of its growth. Thus it leads us to take up towards the record consciously and explicitly the position inevitably held towards it, unconsciously and implicitly, by those who were themselves the products of the process it describes.

So when we say that our Lord presupposed the Old Testament, we must not think that, because the Apostles were not critics, this means that He presupposed what an uncritical English reader would find in the Old Testament. Rather we must say that, because the Apostles were actually the product of the Old Testament, He presupposed in them what a modern critical student finds in the Old Testament, though they would still quite naturally quote particular texts in a wholly uncritical fashion. The greatest gain of the critical study of the Old Testament is that it has restored to us an understanding of the old Scriptures very similar to that which came naturally and inevitably to the later Palestinian Jews.

What then shall we say is the resultant idea of God which the Old Testament, and the history which it describes, created in the minds of those to whom Christ brought His fuller revelation? Plainly a verbal statement of this will be to some extent fallacious, for it was a living whole, and our statement can only set out the various elements within it one by one. But of those elements the chief seem to be these: (1) God is One and Holy, and Holiness includes perfect Righteousness; (2) He is a Living God, not a mere Presence diffused through the world; (3) He is active in History; (4) His righteousness is, in His dealings with us, not only judicial but paternal, and He yearns over His children with love.

(1) *God is One and Holy, and Holiness includes perfect Righteousness.* The conviction that God is One pervades the Old Testament. It is true that various books bring before us stages of development when this position is not yet reached. Thus Jephthah, as represented in the Book of Judges, regards Jehovah as the God of Israel in no other

sense than that in which Chemosh is the God of Moab.[1]
Joshua's farewell to the people traces the belief in One God
back to Abraham,[2] but does not appear to regard other
gods as unreal.[3] The first Commandment of the Decalogue
puts the early faith in a practical form. Whether there are
other gods or not—that question is left open—there is only
one for Israel to serve.

It is at least possible that the truth that there is only
one God was first proclaimed by Amos. Anyhow for all the
prophets from that time onwards this is regarded as a truth
which it is impious to question. The people go on believ-
ing in other gods, not instead of but along with Jehovah,
right down to the Exile.[4] In fact, one main reason why the
Exile is so important a turning-point in the religious
history of Israel is that the people went to Babylon while
this point was still unsettled, but only those who had em-
braced the prophetic faith had the national stability to
return, so that from the Return onwards Monotheism in
the strict sense was finally established. But while it was
the Exile and Return that established it among the people,
it was the realization of the Righteousness of God as He
made Himself known to the prophets which led them to the
assurance of His absolute unity. Abraham had anticipated
this stage of development when he asked, 'Shall not the
Judge of all the earth do right?'[5] When once the will of
God is identified with the Moral Law, Monotheism is
secure.

[1] Judges 11. 23, 24.
[2] Joshua 24. 2, 3.
[3] Ibid., 14.
[4] Cf. e.g. Jeremiah 44.
[5] Genesis 18. 25.

For us this perfect Righteousness is the first suggestion of the term Holiness. But it was not always so. As Rudolf Otto has made quite clear in his most important study called *The Idea of the Holy*, the earliest suggestion of this term is simply awe-inspiring mystery, and it is a great advance when men first find this pre-eminently in the majesty of the Moral Law. At first man bows down in awe before whatever terrifies him. It is the mark of a great step taken when he recognizes that nothing deserves his self-abasement in its presence unless it can command the allegiance of his conscience. Other peoples would have agreed with the mere words 'God is holy'. Only Israel knew that holiness included as its most indispensable element perfect righteousness.

Thus the Unity and the Righteousness of God went together in Israel's apprehension, and not only heightened but transformed the notion of Holiness, which they would have agreed with others in attributing to God. And while this conception of God was only reached with any clear consciousness by the prophets, and only established as the faith of the people by the Exile and Return, yet it absolutely pervades the Old Testament as we know it, because the whole was edited in its present form by adherents of this faith. It may be in part the record of men who held a lower doctrine; but the record itself reflects the convictions of the Prophets and their followers.

(2) *God is a living God.* This is the conviction which most of all distinguishes the Jewish conception of God from the highest results, or at least some of the highest results, of Greek philosophy or Indian Pantheism. Sometimes, no doubt, there is a childlike simplicity in the presentation; but the God of Israel is personal and active as neither

Plato's Idea of Good or Royal Reason, or Aristotle's God eternally thinking thought, or the Hindu Brahma, can be said to be. The God of Israel watches over them, cares for them, is grieved by them. I believe myself that this belief in a living God provides a far more satisfactory philosophy, when once it is accepted, than any of those which represent God as either an indwelling and all-pervasive, but not transcendent, Presence, or those which conceive Him as dwelling apart in untroubled peace, indifferent to the agonies of the world which He has made. But though it provides a satisfactory philosophy, and therein establishes a claim to be accepted as true, I do not think it can be reached by philosophy in any other sense than as the best hypothesis at present available. Certainly it was not by philosophy that Israel reached it.

The crucial doctrine here is that of Creation. The Bible is perfectly clear in its teaching that the world exists by the creative activity of God, who exists Himself independently of His creation. The absolute supremacy of God as Creator is certainly an essential element in the theology of the Old Testament.

(3) *God is active in History.* This is almost identical with the last, but is an aspect of the conception of the living God so fundamental and so distinctive of the Old Testament that it must be mentioned separately. Most of the Old Testament is a history book. But it is a very special kind of history book. It is written to answer a quite different question from that which is in the minds of most historians. Their predominant interest is to answer the questions: What here was the purpose of men? How did this success, or failure, affect that purpose? But the Biblical writers

always have another question in view: What here was the purpose, or the judgment, of God?

There is a very handy illustration in the comparison of the accounts given of two rebellions, both due, so far as men's purposes are concerned, to unpopular taxation. One is the English rebellion against Charles I. The historian sets out to make clear what were the taxes to which objection was taken—Forced Loans, Benevolences, Ship-money. Hampden, on grounds technically constitutional but essentially most irrational,[1] refused to pay ship-money, and so the fight began. You would probably complain rather fiercely of any historian who recorded the events of the reign of Charles I and only glanced at the question of taxation. Yet that is just what the Biblical writer does when he tells you the story of the rebellion against Rehoboam.[2] Of course a little use of imagination will put us on the right track. Solomon had gone in for magnificence; and when kings did that, their subjects had to pay. The House of the Forest of Lebanon is related to the rising of Jeroboam exactly as Versailles is related to the French Revolution. While the great monarch lived, the people endured the burden. When he died, they came to ask his son to make the yoke lighter. You have to guess that the yoke was taxes, until after the king's refusal you get just one hint. 'Rehoboam sent Adoram, who was over the levy; and all Israel stoned him with stones, that he died.' What is the reason for this indifference to the matters that would seem to most historians to be essential? It is that the Biblical writer is not thinking chiefly of what men wanted; he is

[1] That the inland counties ought not to have to pay for the Navy.
[2] I Kings 12. 1-20.

thinking of the purpose and judgment of God. He tells his story to set forth that purpose and judgment so far as his knowledge of God helps him to apprehend these.

The Prophets carry on the same tradition. Isaiah is greatly concerned that the question whether or not Judah should make an alliance with Egypt against Assyria should be decided by reference to God's purposes for His people.[1] But throughout the earlier history and the great prophetic period, Israel and Judah were little nations occupied with almost parochial concerns. With the Exile and the Macedonian invasion the Jews were brought into the sweep of great movements, the rise and fall of vast empires, in face of which their efforts to do more than maintain personal loyalty to Jehovah seemed futile. So Prophecy gives place to Apocalypse, and there is less concern to conform national policy to the divine will, but an even more impressive assertion of the control of history by the over-ruling providence of the Almighty.[2]

(4) *God's righteousness is not only judicial but paternal.* This is hardly apparent in the early stages, and never becomes predominant; but the paternal relationship, broadly speaking, receives increasing emphasis. It is perceptible in the story of Abraham. With Moses it scarcely appears. For example, Moses pleads with Jehovah to deliver His people for the glory of His Name. He never appeals to God's love for them. But in Hosea this feature is strongly marked. The opening verses of his eleventh chapter are classical. 'When Israel was a child, then I loved him, and called my son out

---

[1] Isaiah 30. 1–5, 15–18.

[2] The chief example of Apocalypse in the Old Testament is, of course, the Book of Daniel.

of Egypt; ... I taught Ephraim to walk; I took them on my
arms ... I drew them with cords of a man, with bands of
love.' But in spite of this tenderness, even for Hosea the
judicial relationship is predominant. It is only, I think, in
some of the later Psalms that the paternal relationship
becomes uppermost in the conception of God; but it is so,
for example, in Psalm 103.

> 'The Lord is full of compassion and mercy,
>> Long-suffering and of great goodness.
> He will not alway be chiding;
>> Neither keepeth he his anger for ever.
> He hath not dealt with us after our sins,
>> Nor rewarded us according to our wickednesses.
> For look how high the heaven is in comparison of the earth;
>> So great is his mercy also toward them that fear him.
> Look how wide also the east is from the west;
>> So far hath he set our sins from us.
> Yea, like as a father pitieth his own children,
>> So is the Lord merciful unto them that fear him.
> For he knoweth whereof we are made,
>> He remembereth that we are but dust.' [1]

Here the thought of God is bordering on the Christian
conception.

All of these, and other, elements constituted the
conception of God which was already in the minds of
the Apostles when our Lord first called them to be His disciples. And all this He presupposed. We must not take His
teaching out of its context and regard it as a complete
system by itself. Like all teachers He was bound to give most
attention to the changes that He wished to effect in the
thought of His hearers. Where He was content that they
should merely retain their old idea, He said nothing, but
left the Old Testament to teach them. Whatever we can

[1] Psalm 103. 8–14 (Prayer Book Version).

regard as the real upshot of the Old Testament revelation, that we must say that our Lord presupposes, and accept as part of His own teaching, unless He deliberately modifies it.

Our Lord then presupposed these convictions: that God is exalted in a peerless unity high above all existing things; that His Holiness consists chiefly in His perfect Righteousness; that He is the Creator of the world, not only an indwelling Presence; that He cares for its course and Himself takes action to guide its history; that He watches over His people with a father's care, not only demanding but desiring their obedience. If we want one verse which more than another sums it up, perhaps the best to choose is Isaiah 57. 15: 'Thus saith the high and lofty One that inhabiteth eternity, whose name is Holy; I dwell in the high and holy place, with him also that is of a contrite and humble spirit, to revive the spirit of the humble, and to revive the heart of the contrite ones.'

6

WHAT OUR LORD TAUGHT
BY SPEECH

WE have seen that our Lord was in His teaching always
addressing people to whom the Name of God already conveyed all that the writers of the Old Testament had combined to associate with it. As we turn to His own explicit
teaching we must bear in mind His strong assertion of the
permanency of this revelation—an assertion which He is recorded as making with the utmost emphasis when He was
on the point of giving new doctrine which might otherwise
appear to be a repudiation of the old. 'Think not that I
came to destroy the law, or the prophets: I came not to
destroy, but to fulfil. For verily I say unto you, Till heaven
and earth pass away, one jot or one tittle shall in no wise
pass away from the law till all things be accomplished.'[1]

The Sermon on the Mount is in one most real sense a
correction of the old Law. But it is a correction by way of
completion, not by way of rejection. Perhaps the clearest
illustration of this is found in our Lord's treatment of the
lex talionis—An eye for an eye and a tooth for a tooth. That
principle looks to us like a sanction for vengeance. But
that is a misunderstanding. The essence of the *lex talionis*
is that it sets a limit to the naturally insatiate lust

[1] Matt. 5. 17, 18.

of revenge, which, if left to itself, will take two eyes for an eye and a set of teeth for a tooth. The *lex talionis* allows only such retribution as exactly equals the injury done, forbidding all satisfaction to the indignation felt against the injurer for beginning it. Our Lord was truly fulfilling or completing that process when He said that there should be no retaliation at all.

No doubt the chief reason for His insistence that He was completing and not destroying the Law lay in the fact that He was substituting the spirit for the letter as the source of moral guidance; and men very easily slip into the notion that the spirit is an easier master, more sympathetic and less exacting. But it is not so. A rule can be obeyed, and is then done with; the spirit is never done with. If a rule requires the giving of a tenth of one's worldly goods to God, one can keep the rule and enjoy oneself on what is left. But the spirit requires the dedication of all our goods, so that we never reach the point where we can leave God's claim on one side as satisfied; we are to use all our goods as we believe God would have us use them. Plainly, if we take it seriously, this is a far more exacting demand; but we know how easily we deceive ourselves, and escape from the rule without in any real sense accepting the control of the spirit. Therefore it was that He introduced what may be called the law of the Spirit with the assertion that it completed, and did not destroy, the old Law, and made a greater demand than the most punctilious observers of the old Law were meeting. 'Except your righteousness shall exceed the righteousness of the scribes and Pharisees, ye shall in no wise enter into the kingdom of heaven.'[1]

[1] Matt. 5. 20.

St Peter, we remember, wanted to have a rule to live by in that matter of forgiveness, on which his Master laid so terrifying an emphasis. He wanted to know what was the point when he might say, as we always want to say, 'Well, I have overlooked his deceiving me three times and have been ready to help him again; but I don't think I can be expected to go on.' Three times is perhaps about as much as our conscience usually requires. St Peter was prepared for more than this, for there could be no doubt the Master did require a great deal in this respect; would seven times do? No, it would not. We are to forgive till seventy times seven, or (as no one could possibly count the injuries inflicted on him by one person up to four hundred and ninety) as often as we are injured.[1] A rule can be obeyed, so that we are then left free; but the spirit is constant and always requires action along the same lines; the spirit of forgiveness tells us to forgive every time. Truly the spirit is more exacting than the letter can ever be.

All of this may seem to be irrelevant to our purpose, which is to consider, not our Lord's ethical teaching, but His teaching about God. It helps us, however, in approaching that theme, to realize how completely and explicitly He did presuppose the Old Testament. But the points which I have selected in illustration of that theme have also this special relevance, that they turn out on investigation to be, in fact, rooted in the conviction of the absolute and all-embracing sovereignty of God. For the penetrating and pervasive authority of the spirit is the moral aspect of a God whose overruling Providence nothing escapes; and this is the first point which I wish to mention in our Lord's

[2] Matt. 18. 21, 22.

teaching about God. For with no more introduction I propose now to pass on to those elements in that teaching which seem to me most conspicuous.

(1) First, I should put the assumption of *God's absolute supremacy*. No words can exaggerate the degree to which this everywhere determines our Lord's outlook upon the world and human life. There is, of course, nothing in the Gospels which remotely resembles a philosophic argument for the Being of God. It is even misleading to say that this is assumed, though being accepted without argument it is, of course, intellectually regarded, an assumption. But the intellectual aspect is very subordinate. God is for Jesus of Nazareth not an idea but a fact, and a fact incomparably more sure than any other. It is impossible to quote texts about this; from the nature of the case, it appears as a universally controlling influence, not as a special tenet. Perhaps it is rash to say that men only assert absolute certainty when they have doubts which they wish to quiet, but it would not be far from the truth. When Cardinal Newman says that for him there were, at any rate at one stage, only two luminous points of certainty—God and his own soul—I get a conviction that this was only so at certain times of exaltation, and that at other times he was even more acutely conscious of the physical world, his own body, his friends, his plans, Monsignor Talbot at the Vatican, and so forth. We do not affirm our primary certainties, at least as a general rule; they appear as a universal background of all our affirmations. Such is the assurance of the reality of God in the teaching of our Lord. Nothing is ever conceived except in its relation to God. Other facts may be omitted from consideration—trifles like the Roman Empire,

or the possibility of capsize in a boat on a rough lake; but God is never for one moment absent from thought. It is God first, God last, and God all the time between.

Moreover, there is no assertion in set terms that God controls the world; but this is so much a part of the very meaning of His Name that the thought is as pervasive as the thought of God Himself. But it is surely characteristic that it is rather on God's care for the very little things than on His power over the very great things that our Lord loves to dwell. Perhaps this is because His power over the great things had been made familiar by the Old Testament; it was His care for the little things that needed to be brought home. 'Are not five sparrows sold for two farthings? and not one of them is forgotten in the sight of God. But the very hairs of your head are all numbered.'[1] It is God who feeds the birds and clothes the grass of the field. We cannot imagine our Lord saying, as St Paul once did, 'Is it for the oxen that God careth?'[2] And all this reaches its culmination in our Lord's teaching about children—perhaps the most startlingly original of all His doctrines. No doubt He Himself loved children, but His teaching reflects much more than His human love for them; it has its root in His assurance of God's care for them.

In all these passages the note is tenderness, not the severity which is more easily suggested to our minds by the term sovereignty or supremacy. To the aspect of severity we shall come back. But we must not let the tenderness of God's care for the little things in His creation obscure the fact that this implies a truly universal sovereignty even

[1] Luke 12. 6, 7; cf. Matt. 10. 29, 30.
[2] I Cor. 9. 9.

more impressively than does the control of the general course of history by an Almighty Ruler.

(2) Closely connected with this thought of a universal supremacy of God, shown especially in care for the little things in creation, is *the sense of intimate relation between the Natural and the Moral Law*. Both alike are regarded quite simply as God's Will, and both alike are regarded as evidences of His character. Here again we are on Old Testament ground. To Israel all natural phenomena were activities of God, and the Laws of Nature and of Duty have never been more impressively co-related than in Psalm 19, where, as in Wordsworth's *Ode to Duty*, the passage is direct from the movements of the heavenly bodies, as they declare the glory of God, to that undefiled law which converts the soul and gives wisdom to the simple. But in parables and illustrations our Lord presses this implication of God's universal sovereignty to a length elsewhere unparalleled. Everyone who stops to think at all as he reads the New Testament must see how constantly He uses the ordinary processes of Nature as illustrations of God's method, with the implication that His method in the moral sphere must be the same. But sometimes we find something more emphatic than parables; nothing can be more explicit than the evidence that God is 'kind toward the unthankful and evil'[1] afforded by the sun and the rain. 'Love your enemies, and pray for them that persecute you; that ye may be sons of your Father which is in heaven: for he maketh his sun to rise on the evil and the good, and sendeth rain on the just and the unjust.'[2]

[1] Luke 6. 35.
[2] Matt. 5. 44, 45.

This leads us to the most distinctive element in our Lord's teaching about God. But before we pass on to that we must notice His occasional warnings that we cannot interpret any particular occurrences in the light of our limited knowledge of God's purposes. The believer who prays, and receives the boon for which he prays, will naturally connect the two. But he cannot prove that the boon was not coming to him anyhow. There is, however, little harm in too easily attributing what we welcome to the direct and special activity of God, so long as we avoid all tendency to suppose ourselves His favourites. The danger comes when men attribute to the direct and special activity of God untoward events, especially those which befall other people. It is very hazardous to see God coming in judgment when calamities come to ourselves or to others—specially to others, for this tends to self-righteousness. So we are warned not to think the victims of cruelty or of accidents specially wicked, or that their sufferings are a divinely inflicted punishment.[1] No doubt all that happens falls within God's purpose and those who seek and follow that purpose will find how even what seems evil gives opportunities to fulfil it.[2] But we do not know enough of that purpose either in its range or in its detail to acclaim any event, especially any event that involves suffering, as a direct result of the divine activity. We must not say of earthquakes or of military defeats, 'Lo, here!' or 'Lo, there!'[3] Our concern with God's purpose is not to understand its universal range, but to find and obey that in it which concerns ourselves, confident

[1] Luke 13. 1-5.
[2] John 9. 1-3.
[3] Luke 17. 24.

that if we are really trying to live in His obedience and fellowship, all things, even those which in themselves are evil, will become occasions of good.

(3) We come now to something which is so great an extension of anything in the Old Testament, and so complete a readjustment of its whole balance, as to be completely original. This is our Lord's insistence on *the indiscriminate love of God*. The chief passage is that lately quoted about the sun and the rain. But it pervades the whole Gospel. Amos had long ago extended what Israel had learnt of God's guidance of history to other nations besides Israel. God did, indeed, care for Israel, but He cared equally for the Ethiopians; He had indeed brought Israel out of Egypt, but so too had He brought the Philistines from Caphtor and the Syrians from Kir.[1] But though He had equal care for them all, it was rather as a King demanding from all His due than as a Father watching over them all with love. Moreover, the extension of belief in God's all-ruling Providence was demanded by the realization of His Unity. If there is only one God, that God must have control of all nations. But what our Lord teaches goes far beyond all this. It is not only that God declares Himself to all peoples and from all demands obedience, rewarding and punishing all alike as they give or withhold their obedience; He is now declared to love all alike, whether they obey or disobey. St Paul plainly feels this to be a truly revolutionary disclosure.[2] God, as Jesus Christ teaches us to understand Him, loves all His children with an unquenchable love. They may ignore Him, betray Him, defy Him; they may in ways

[1] Amos 9. 7.
[2] Romans 5. 6–8.

innumerable wound His love. But He always goes on loving them, with a love undiminished by their ingratitude.

In one sense we are so familiar with this element in Christ's teaching, that a re-statement of it has a platitudinous air. In another sense, we are so far from appreciating its real significance that its implications are utterly unperceived even by those who would most loudly assert its familiarity. For what is here at stake is the whole of the relation of religion to morality. There is a long tradition in human thought, according to which the very existence of God is chiefly established by His vindication of the Moral Law. The most conspicuous representative of this tradition is the great philosopher Kant. But this seems, at first sight, to be imperilled by a declaration that God's love for the wicked is no less than His love for the (comparatively) righteous. No doubt Kant is more concerned with the need for securing the association of happiness with goodness than with that of ensuring the punishment of the wicked. But even so, and even granting that love for the wicked may show itself in punishing them, it is very hard to fit such a saying as that about the sun and the rain into the context of the *Metaphysic of Ethics*.

That a religious doctrine should apparently conflict with a great tradition of human thought is a serious matter. What is more serious is that this tradition is itself central and pivotal for the Old Testament. That Ethical Monotheism which is the distinctive doctrine of Israel rests on the faith in God as vindicator of righteousness, by the preservation of the righteous and the destruction of the wicked. We are indeed assured that God takes no pleasure in the

death of the sinner;[1] and we have repeated expressions of
the love wherewith He waits and longs for their return to
obedience. But this is still subordinate. Pre-eminently He
is King and Judge. Even if it were admitted that He was
conceived as grieving over those whom He destroys, there
can be no doubt that this indiscriminate bounty to evil and
good alike is foreign to the thought of the Old Testament,
and at first sight destructive of its whole scheme of doctrine.

But in fact our Lord is here, too, completing and not
destroying the Law. For the whole purpose of the Law and
of its punishments is not to secure that the wicked are
punished, but to keep people from wickedness by the fear
of punishment. We always get our whole conception of Law
wrong if we think of it only in relation to those who are
proved guilty of breaking it. Far the greater part of its influence is exerted in checking people from doing what it
forbids. Mr N. P. Birley, in a recent textbook of English
History between 1660 and 1714, says of the provision
concerning the removal of unworthy judges in the Act of
Settlement of 1701: 'This enactment has been so effective
that it has never been necessary to use it.' Indeed it is true
that if a Law perfectly attains its object, no one will ever be
prosecuted under it. For its object is to prevent the commis-
sion of some crime; and if that object is attained, that crime
is never committed.

When people clamour for the vindication of the Moral
Law by the punishment of the wicked, they always think
of the wicked as being someone else. They are not demanding the condign punishment of their own sins. But the only
right way to inquire what is the moral influence of any

[1] Ezekiel 18. 32.

conception of God, is for the inquirer to ask what is its effect upon him. Undoubtedly this influence mainly consists in the unconscious tendency of every worshipper to imitate his God. If the God be conceived as vindictive, the worshipper will become vindictive. But that is to fix him in the self-centredness from which above all things he needs to be delivered. But if the God be conceived as universal love, the worshipper will tend to become more and more unselfish and loving. Further, it is in the thought of God's love for him that each worshipper finds his highest incentive to goodness; and just when he fails to find it insufficient to carry him over some cause of special alienation, and when he would indulge his dislike if he could possibly regard the object of his dislike as being in the disfavour of God, he is carried on to real love even of an enemy by the recollection that God loves that enemy as truly as himself.

So soon then as I escape from the Pharisaic attitude of thinking what my conscience requires that God should do to someone else, and reach the Christian temper which asks what God wishes to do with me, I find that the apparently non-moral doctrine of God's indiscriminate love is precisely that which alone can give me the new energy of righteousness which I need.

(4) The doctrine of God's indiscriminate love finds its fullest expression in *our Lord's teaching about forgiveness*. The Parable of the Prodigal Son[1] makes it perfectly clear that God is always ready to receive back into His favour His self-willed children. It is true that the Prodigal had first to come to himself and set out on the homeward journey

[1] Luke 15. 11-32.

before he could be received. But that was in the nature of the case. The Father did nothing to keep him away till certain conditions were fulfilled. It is often said that our Lord's doctrine is that of free forgiveness on the sole condition of repentance; but if by forgiveness is meant the readiness and desire to restore the old relations of love and intimacy, then there are no conditions at all. God always and unceasingly desires to maintain those relations and to restore them as soon as ever we break them. But there is a condition that we must fulfil if we are to make our own the forgiveness which God always and freely offers. And it is noticeable that repentance is not, in fact, mentioned in this connection. The one thing that is mentioned, and that with a most solemn reiteration, is our forgiveness of those who have injured us or are in our debt. The prayer for forgiveness is the only petition in the Lord's Prayer to which any condition is attached; and it is this condition. The lesson is driven home by the Parable of the Unforgiving Servant;[1] and part of the significance of this is concealed by our unfamiliarity with the monetary terms employed. The debt which the king was ready to forgive was about two and a half million pounds—such a debt as could never be repaid, so that the plea, 'Have patience with me, and I will pay thee all,' was certainly an idle one. But the debt which that same servant refused to forgive was about £5, which might easily be repaid. For indeed our debt to God is infinite and cannot be repaid; to Him we owe every moment of our time and every ounce of our strength, so that even if we are utterly devoted for the future without fault or defect, that cannot make good our failures in the

[1] Matt. 18. 23–25.

past. But He freely forgives, unless we block His forgiveness by our refusal to forgive the comparatively trifling injuries which are all that our fellow-men can do to us. But that refusal is fatal.

This is not hard to understand. Forgiveness does not mean remission of penalty, but restoration to the old relationship of children with our Father. But He cannot restore us to His own intimacy if we decline to be on brotherly terms with His other children. If in a family one member has quarrelled with his father and with the rest, the father may long to have him back, but he cannot do so unless he can be friends with the others. Or, to put the matter more theologically, forgiveness is restoration to fellowship with God; and God is love; to be in fellowship with God is therefore to be filled with the spirit of love, and in so far as we remain unloving towards anyone we shut ourselves out from the fellowship of God.

I am at present attending only to what Christ taught by speech; the next lecture will supplement this by calling attention to what He taught by action. So we shall come to the connection between His Death and our forgiveness. But the upshot of His spoken teaching surely is this: God bears no resentment; you may by the sinful state of your will enter into antagonism against God, and then, of course, He is your antagonist; but that is of your choice, not His, and He always desires that change in you which will end His antagonism; one condition, and only one, He makes, but that is utterly indispensable—it is that you extend to others the same forgiveness that you seek from Him.

(5) What has been said about love and forgiveness is

gathered up in the doctrine of *God's Fatherhood*. The use of the term was not new, but the intensity of meaning which our Lord put into it was so new that men felt bound to keep the Aramaic word that He used even when they were writing Greek. That surely is the explanation of the phrase, 'Abba, Father'.[1] Everywhere we are to interpret our relations to God and His dealings with us in the light of this family relationship. So we get beyond any notions of anything like legal justice either as between God and man or as between one man and another in His sight. The main point of the Parable of the Unjust Judge is, no doubt, the need for that undaunted faith of which persistent prayer is the expression; but it also strongly implies that people who will think of God as Judge, instead of thinking of Him as Father, and Judge only so far as a father is a judge to his children, will find Him acting on very unjudicial principles.[2]

So too the Parable of the Labourers in the Vineyard, in addition to its main lesson, seems to say that if we will treat God as an employer or taskmaster, and not as our father, He will seem most arbitrary.[3] But here the main point is very relevant. St Peter had just asked what reward the disciples might expect for all that they had left to follow Christ. The answer is that they will indeed receive most abundant reward; but if they are in the frame of mind which looks for rewards proportioned to service rendered, they will be disappointed. Then comes the story of the labourers hired at different times; of how the employer

[1] Mark 14. 36; Rom. 8. 15; Gal. 4. 6.
[2] Luke 18. 1–8.
[3] Matt. 20. 1–16.

specially arranged that they should be paid in reverse order, so that when those who had only worked for one hour received the full day's wage, the hopes of the others were sure to be raised; of the disappointment which they felt when they received the same, and of the employer's justification of his act by reference to his arbitrary will. Of course, it is all wrong in relations between an employer and labourers. But, of course, it is all right in the family. The oldest child does not complain because the youngest has an equal share of the parents' love, or claim larger presents because he has been obedient for a longer time. So it is in our service of God. He rewards those who serve Him well, but no question of justice between Him and us, or between ourselves in His sight, can ever arise if we properly understand the situation; He is our Father and we are His children. This is a realm quite other than the world of claims and counter-claims to which justice belongs.

(6) But *God is King as well as Father*; indeed the world to which Christ points us is one where the Father is King and the King is Father. All that is said about the Kingdom of God reminds us of that Divine Sovereignty which our Lord presupposed as already taught by the Old Testament. And while we know that the Father desires us to approach Him gladly, we on our side cannot approach the King except with reverence. And in this reverence there must be found what the Old Testament means by 'the fear of the Lord.' This is not just fright of what He may do to us, which is a purely selfish and, if chronic, a demoralizing emotion; it is the sense of unworthiness and littleness and helplessness before the All-holy and All-mighty. To men brought up on the Old Testament there was little need to

dwell on this; but we must remind ourselves that our Lord, far from repudiating this, reinforced it in very terrible words. We are to remember that there is a fear due to God which can never be due to our worst enemy on earth. 'I say unto you, my friends, Be not afraid of them which kill the body, and after that have no more that they can do. But I will warn you whom ye shall fear: Fear him, which after he hath killed hath authority to cast into hell; yea, I say unto you, fear him.'[1]

(7) This naturally leads us to the thought of *Judgment*, many aspects of which lie beyond our present scope. But we must not dwell on the indiscriminate love and free forgiveness of God without supplementing this by His terrible severity as our Lord teaches us to know Him. For those who try and trust there is His gracious promise; but for those who either do not try, or who proudly rely on their own righteous will, there is dreadful warning. The love of God is not a sentimental readiness to give us what we happen to want; it is a passionate yearning to raise us to its own likeness, knowing that this is best for us; and, therefore, for very love's sake, God will be relentlessly stern against all in us that is self-centred; our lower nature and unconverted hearts are likely often to think Him cruel. If you are not perfect in love, and still do not tremble before God, you have not understood the God and Father of our Lord Jesus Christ. What are the words of Incarnate Love on the threshold of the Passion wherein His Love was most perfectly revealed? 'The stone which the builders rejected, the same was made the head of the

[1] Luke 12. 4, 5; cf. Matt. 10. 28.

corner. Every one that falleth on that stone shall be broken to pieces; but on whomsoever it shall fall, it will scatter him as dust.'[1]

Because God is Love, He desires the answering love of His children; but that must be freely given, for otherwise it is not love at all. Therefore, because God is love, He gives us the awful responsibility of freedom. We are free, if we so choose, to repel His love. We may even do this with such completeness, according to the most natural interpretation of Christ's words, that we are shut out utterly from His Presence; that is Hell. And if we believe in Hell, it is because we believe so completely in the love of God.

(8) This responsibility of freedom would be an impossible burden were it not for the last point which I propose to mention in our Lord's teaching about God; this is *the Gift of the Spirit*. Hitherto my references have been almost entirely to the Synoptic Gospels; now our main concern is with the Fourth. But for our present purpose this need cause no misgiving on critical grounds, whatever we may think about the historic value of the Fourth Gospel, for the main point is contained in the Synoptic Gospels also.[2] Plainly we cannot go into one of the main doctrines of the Christian faith at this point. But the promise of Christ is clear. If a man opens his heart to the Father's love as made known through the human life of the Son, he finds within himself and in the fellowship of his co-disciples a power of answering love and service which is more than his own, and which at last if not at first he recognizes as the Holy Spirit. God loves and calls us to an answering love; but we

[1] Luke 20. 17, 18; cf. Matt. 21. 42, 44.
   Luke 11. 13; 12. 12.

are not left to offer the unworthy response of which alone we are capable; the love with which we answer is God Himself within us.

WHAT OUR LORD TAUGHT
BY ACTION

As the first missionaries went about their work, no doubt they left behind them some record of our Lord's utterances, so that their converts should have, as far as possible in His own words, the principles of the life to which by Baptism the converts were committed. In fact there seems to be good reason for thinking that the earliest part of the material now contained in the Synoptic Gospels was a collection of the sayings of the Lord; the matter common to the First and Third Gospels, but not given by St Mark, is generally supposed to come from an early source used by both evangelists. This is called 'Q', and it consists almost entirely of teaching. And, as I have said, it is very likely the earliest of all the material which has been worked up into the Synoptic Gospels.

But while it is likely that the Lord's spoken teaching was the first part of the Gospels to be written, there can be no doubt at all that His Life and Death played a greater part than His words in converting souls. St Paul may have left copies of 'Q' or some similar document behind him when he left a city where he had preached. But his preaching, by his own testimony, concerned the Cross and Resurrec-

tion rather than the Sermon on the Mount. He proclaimed
a crucified Messiah rather than a supreme religious teacher.
And in his Epistles he scarcely refers to the ethical teaching
of the Lord, while he dwells constantly on His Death and
Resurrection from the dead. It is when we turn to what our
Lord taught by action that we reach what all the saints
have found to be the heart of His revelation of God.

But here we presuppose the Incarnation, which is the
central doctrine of the Christian faith. Always remember
that the real meaning of that doctrine is not to be found
in what it affirms concerning a historical person—Jesus of
Nazareth—but in what it affirms concerning the Eternal
God. The religious interest, if that expression may be
allowed, of asserting the Deity of Christ is found in the
consequent faith that God, the Eternal and Almighty, is
like Jesus Christ, that His character is the character of
Jesus Christ. Here we assume that doctrine, and can go on
to consider some of our Lord's actions in the light of His
declaration, 'He that hath seen me hath seen the Father.'[1]

(1) We begin with *the threefold Temptation*. No doubt
the record of this comes from our Lord Himself, for He was
alone at the time. The story is His own statement (of course
in parable form) of the problem which confronted Him
when at His Baptism He knew that He was called to begin
His work as Messiah. There were various forms of Messianic expectation, and no doubt many devout Jews held
them all at once, as popular religion commonly combines a
large assortment of incompatible beliefs. There is no harm
in this, so long as it is only the figures and metaphors which
are incompatible, not the substance behind them. But He

[1] John 14. 9; cf. Col. 1. 15; Heb. 1. 3.

who was actually to do the Messianic work of inaugurating the Kingdom of God must of necessity adopt some one method. Now broadly speaking the old conceptions all rested on, or at least contained, some element either of bribery or of force. The Messianic banquet[1] suggested an appeal to men's love of comfort and luxury; the King who should rule in perfect righteousness from the throne of David[2] suggested the use of such compulsion as is part of the machinery of all earthly governments; the appearance of the Son of Man on the clouds of heaven[3] suggested such a display of unquestionable authority that doubt or resistance would be inconceivable. Now these are precisely the methods which our Lord rejected at the outset of His ministry.[4] He would not use His power wherewith as Messiah He was endowed, to satisfy His own wants or those of others as a means to establishing His Kingdom; He would not adopt the methods of the Prince of this world to win the world for His Kingdom; He would not give the 'sign from heaven' which would make all doubt of His divine mission impossible.

That is so far, of course, a purely negative result. But, like all negatives, it rests on a positive basis. These methods were rejected because they were all incompatible with what turns out to be the one foundation of the Kingdom—the free response of human hearts and consciences and wills to the appeal of perfect love. At present the way is made clear for this, but that is all. Before we go on, however, it is worth while to notice that the thought of compelling men to

1 Isaiah 25. 6; cf. Luke 14. 15.
2 Isaiah 9. 6, 7.
3 Daniel 7. 13, 14.
4 Luke 4. 1-12; Matt. 4. 1-10.

accept Christ's authority had to be constantly repudiated, for the disciples had not abandoned it. A striking illustration occurs in the scene where the sons of Zebedee wished to call down fire from heaven on the Samaritans who would not receive Him.[1] Just before His arrest our Lord was conscious of the possibility of summoning celestial aid against His captors.[2] But most impressive of all is His treatment of Judas. The Lord knew what was in his mind. He had given the directions to the two disciples, who were to prepare the Last Supper, in a kind of cypher[3]—presumably so that the traitor should not know and bring the soldiers there. At that Supper He says that one of them will betray Him; so Judas knew that he was detected. It would have been easy to give the name and bid the disciples act; there were, we know, two swords in that room,[4] or we may be sure that Peter and the two Sons of Thunder would have been ready to bind the traitor there while the Lord escaped. But He only gave the hint, which explained His action, to the beloved disciple.[5] To the traitor, who knew himself detected, He made the appeal of love by singling him out for especial honour.[6] That appeal, so made, must soften his heart or harden it. It hardened it, and the beloved disciple saw the fact in his face.[7] The Lord saw it too, but still refused to go back from love to force; He would have no unwilling disciples; if a chosen friend chose to be a traitor,

[1] Luke 9. 51–56.
[2] Matt. 26. 52, 53.
[3] Mark 14. 12–16; Luke 22. 7–13.
[4] Luke 22. 38.
[5] John 13. 21–26.
[6] John 13. 26.
[7] John 13. 27.

a traitor let him be: 'That thou doest, do quickly.'[1] And Judas passed out under the Lord's protecting silence.

Now remember: what we are watching is not merely the mutual dealings of two persons who lived long ago. We are watching the revelation once for all of the Eternal God in His dealing with the souls of men. He still appeals to us as our Father in the name of His love; we may reject that appeal if we will. If, called to be sons, we choose to be traitors, we may. Is it not true that there is nothing so merciless as the love of God? For indeed it would seem like mercy that He should forcibly prevent Judas—or me—from betraying Him. Yes—mercy to that lower and weaker self in us which asks love to be indulgent. But God pays us the terrible compliment of appealing always to what is best in us and never overrides our freedom.

There is judgment, truly, as we saw in considering our Lord's spoken teaching. When He calls by kindness and we will not hear, He calls by judgment, to give us a new chance that way. But even though the judgment brings bitter suffering, He still will not force us to learn its lesson. All our Lord's dealings with men declare this fact concerning God: *God respects men's freedom to the uttermost, even though they use it to wound Him and to destroy themselves.*

(2) We find an application of this principle and much else besides when we come to consider our Lord's *Miracles*. Here I wish to call attention to three points:

(a) *He never appeals to His miracles as evidence of His authority, but, on the contrary, deprecates the public interest which they excite.* Possessed of power and con-

[1] John 13. 27.

fronted with need, love cannot but use the power to satisfy the need. So He heals those who are diseased. But He often tells them to say nothing about it. And when, after a great number had been healed in Capernaum, the excitement rose very high, He withdrew for solitary prayer in the night; and to St Peter, no doubt elated by the signs of public interest, and bringing the news that all were seeking Him, He replied, 'Let us go elsewhere into the next towns, that I may proclaim [the Kingdom] there also.'[1] As He goes a leper comes and asks for healing. The Lord heals him, but charges him sternly to tell no one; the word translated 'sternly' or 'strictly' suggests anger; this further healing was contrary to His purpose.[2]

Now we have here a balance of considerations which it is important to hold steadily. In the first place, the Lord does heal men's bodily ills; there is no suggestion that these represent the will of God in such sense that they ought to be passively endured, or that to cure men's physical condition is other than spiritual work. But in the second place all this is incidental; the main purpose is to proclaim the Kingdom of God, and public excitement about miraculous cures is regarded as a hindrance to the growth of the spiritual work for which Christ came. Or in other words God wills our health and all else that is for our temporal welfare; but He does not put this first; and if we put it first, or come to Him chiefly for such boons as these, we misunderstand both Him and His gift.

(b) *The miracles of Christ are an assertion of the subordination of the physical to the spiritual.* We make a great

[1] Mark 1. 35–38.
[2] Mark 1. 40–44.

mistake when we speak of them as breaches of Natural Law. A law of Nature affirms that a particular cause must have a particular effect. Here we have an unusual cause and an unusual effect. This is no breach of any law of Nature; each miracle is an instance of a law of which there may be no other instances. But, in fact, our Lord teaches us to regard His miracles, for the most part at least, as illustrations of a law of which we can ourselves make use.[1] But the condition of success is of course the reality of our devotion. Nature is God's creation; it is when our wills are the channels of God's Purpose that they can control the physical world. Our Lord's human will was always thus the channel of God's Purpose.

(c) But the chief characteristic of our Lord's miracles remains to be noticed; it is *the subordination of power to love*. Perhaps we grasp this best by the help of the inquiry made by John the Baptist and our Lord's answer.[2] St John the Baptist had launched a great movement which had profoundly shaken the nation. He made much more stir in his own lifetime than our Lord made in His earthly ministry. He was an embodiment of power, even though he worked no miracles. And he had recognized our Lord as one greater, even immeasurably greater, than himself, and had spoken of Him as the Lamb of God which beareth away the sin of the world.[3] Then had come his imprisonment; and in his prison he heard about the works of this greater follower. And it was those works which made him doubt. It was 'when John heard in the prison

---

[1] John 14. 12.
[2] Luke 7. 18–35; Matt. 11. 2–19.
[3] Mark 1. 7; Luke 3. 15–17; Matt. 3. 11, 12; John 1. 19–36; 3. 27–30.

the works of the Christ' that he sent to ask whether what he hoped was true after all. For nothing was happening of the kind that changes the course of history. There were some blind men who could see, some deaf men who could hear, a few dead folk who were alive again, and a number of poor people cheered by good news. Could this be the way that the Kingdom of God would come?

The answer is merely to put before John again the facts which had caused his anxiety, with the significant addition, 'Blessed is he that is not scandalized at me.' Then the people are told that John is indeed a prophet and the greatest of the prophets; yet the least in the Kingdom of God is greater. What does all this suggest? Certainly it suggests that somewhere in these works is to be found the evidence of divine presence. St John the Baptist is so far above the level of the crowd as to be free from their excitement at the wonder of the miracles that, on the contrary, they seem to him an insufficient display of the divine power. But he is still below the level of the Kingdom. For what, after all, is the most striking feature of our Lord's miracles? It is that *power is always subordinate to love*. Having this power, He never uses it for Himself, nor to impose His will on others, but always and only in giving service. This is the divine use of power; and to realize that in God's order, and in His dealings with men, power is always subordinate to love, is to grasp the distinctive element in the Christian doctrine of God, the fundamental principle of the Kingdom of God.

(3) It was especially at the end of His ministry that our Lord taught by action. After He had been recognized freely by St Peter at Caesarea Philippi, He began for the first time

to say what was *the Messianic act by which He would inaugurate the Kingdom of God,* namely, that He should 'suffer many things, and be rejected by the elders, and the chief priests and the scribes, and be killed, and after three days rise again.'[1] And at once He started on the journey to Jerusalem which ended on Calvary. But first, as it were in preparation, He gave Himself to that ecstasy of communion with the Father which is set before us in the story of the *Transfiguration,* wherein the Head of the Law and the Head of the Prophets spake with Him of the Exodus —for Him 'decease', for His people deliverance—which He should accomplish at Jerusalem.[2] So He prepared Himself, and His closest friends, for the journey and its climax. As they went He strode before them with something in His manner that amazed and terrified them.[3] Arrived in the neighbourhood of Jerusalem He deliberately fulfilled Zechariah's prophecy by entering in triumph riding upon an ass, thereby at once claiming Messiahship and indicating that His Messiahship was peaceful and based on humility.[4] Arrived there, He purges the Temple courts, interfering on His own authority with a commerce which had the sanction of custom and was conducted under the auspices of, and largely for the profit of, the High Priest.[5] In all of these we see the *claim to divine authority coupled with a complete absence of self-concern.* As we see God in Jesus

[1] Mark 8. 27–31; Luke 9. 18–22; Matt. 16. 13–21. For the word 'freely' in the text cf. Matt. 16. 17.

[2] Mark 9. 2–8; Luke 9. 28–36 (the word 'Exodus' is in 5. 31); Matt. 17. 1–8.

[3] Mark 10. 32.

[4] Mark 11. 1–10; Luke 19. 29–40; Matt. 21. 1–11; John 12. 12–19; Zech. 9. 9.

[5] Mark 11. 15–18, 27–33; Luke 19. 45–20. 8; Matt. 21. 12–14, 23–27.

Christ we learn to believe in Him as absolutely sovereign by right and by power, yet always making His claim for the sake of the people to whom He makes it, never for any satisfaction of Himself except the satisfaction which love finds in answering love.

(4) So we come to the *Last Supper*. The order of events is not quite clear. I have already spoken of the last appeal made to the traitor-disciple. In all the wealth of material for meditation in that whole episode I will now mention only two points.

(*a*) The first is *the washing of the disciples' feet*.[1] It was, so St John had learnt to realize, in a special consciousness of His Deity—'knowing that the Father had given all things into his hands, and that he came forth from God and went unto God'—that He performed the act of menial service. Thus God—the Eternal, Almighty, Glorious God —serves His children. It is a supreme revelation of the divine humility. And to accept it calls for a complete humility in men. St Peter at first is horrified; then, when he is told that loyalty involves acceptance, he wants to ask for more than is offered. The last resort of human pride is to attribute a proud dignity to the object of its worship. But even that has to go. In the light of Christ's revelation no place is left for pride at all. *When God comes among men, it is as their servant*.[2]

(*b*) The other episode at the Last Supper which imperatively claims our attention is the first Eucharist.[3] We must not now go into any difficult questions. Nor are we at the moment concerned with the teaching here given with

[1] John 13. 1–10.
[2] Cf. Mark 10. 42–45; Luke 22. 24–27.
[3] I Cor. 11. 23-25; Mark 14. 22-25; Luke 22. 14-20. Matt. 26. 26-29.

regard to the nature and implications of our discipleship. We are concerned only to ask, What here do we learn about God? The answer is simple and is in line with all the rest of our Lord's teaching about God. It is this: *God gives Himself, at any cost to Himself, to be the life of our souls, if we will have it so.* Our Lord took the Bread, of which He said that it was His Body; He gave thanks for it, He blessed it, He broke it, He gave it. So our Lord, we know, was treating His Body. When He let Judas go, He condemned Himself (humanly speaking) to the Passion. Because Judas was then in His power, His Death was a voluntary sacrifice.[1] That is why the life-giving sacrifice is for evermore associated with 'the same night in which He was betrayed.'

(5) By His action at the Last Supper our Lord gave His disciples the clue whereby to understand *the Passion.* His deeds and words together had been plainly sacrificial. He had spoken of a new convenant between God and Man, ratified, as the old covenant had been, with blood; but the new covenant was ratified with His own Blood. So He led them to understand that His Death, which had the appearance of an execution, was in reality a sacrifice. But the victim offered in the sacrifice was no symbolic substitute; it was Himself.

If it was impossible in these lectures to attempt any real discussion of the doctrines of the Holy Spirit or the Eucharist, still more is it impossible to attempt here any discussion of the Atonement. But again we remember that we are not now concerned with the human side of our faith, but with Christ's revelation of God. What do we learn

[1] Cf. John 10. 17, 18.

from the Passion of our Lord concerning God? Out of all that might be said I choose three points.

(a) *In the Passion and Cross of Christ we see what our sin means to God.* We naturally think of Him as indignant against sin; and this, of course, is right as far as it goes. But behind the indignation is the agony of love repelled. And He is willing to bear all that we inflict. When He is reviled, He reviles not again; when He suffers, He threatens not.[1] It is right to change the past tense to the present if what we watch as we gaze upon the Cross is not a mere historic episode, but the revelation at a moment of the Eternal God. And let us remember that it was not the sins which men call disreputable that brought Christ to the Cross. The outcasts of society had no quarrel against Him. It was the highly respectable sins of religious conservatism, of political ambition, of financial self-interest. What costs God such agony as only the Cross could reveal is not the monumental wickedness of a few monsters of iniquity, but just the sins that all of us indulge in more or less. There we see what each one of us is costing God.

(b) Because we see in the Passion what our sin costs God, *we see there also the righteousness of God and the self-sacrifice involved in His free forgiveness.* Christ's doctrine of free forgiveness by itself would be open to the charge that it represented God as indifferent to moral conduct, and that it therefore was demoralizing to men. But by showing us what sin means to God, our Lord refuted that charge before it could be made. If sin causes Him such pain, that is proof of the depth of the antagonism between His nature and sin. Nor can anyone be encouraged by God's free for-

[1] Peter 2. 23.

giveness to make light of his sin when he sees in the Cross the measure of its evil. The love which freely forgives those who inflict such agony is not an easy-going amiability, nor can it do other than brace the wills of those on whom, in neglect of its own injuries, it bestows forgiveness.

(c) God made the world, and gave men the freedom which they have used to devastate the world. *Here we see God bearing, and by bearing destroying, the evil in the world.* The Cross represents the worst that evil could do; nothing in principle worse than the rejection and crucifixion of the Lord of love can ever happen. But through all the ages it has been by the Cross that Christ has destroyed the evil in men's hearts and in the world. Sin brought Christ to the Cross, and by the Cross Christ destroys sin. So what we find here is God bearing the load of the world's evil and, by bearing, destroying it. He enters into the very depth of our misery and helplessness. In the cry from the Cross, 'My God, my God, why didst thou forsake me?'[1] we seem to see him emerging from an agony where it appeared that God had failed Himself; so utterly does He accept all, and worse than all, that we can know of the load of evil. The self-sacrifice is absolute and without reserve. But by that sacrifice He abolishes the evil which caused the agony, and we find that the innermost secret of the heart of Godhead is triumphant sacrifice.

(6) For the Cross was not the end. It was real, and all for which it stands must be eternally true of God. But it is not the whole of the truth. Historically there can be no doubt that the Church of Christ rests not on the Cross but on *the Resurrection.* The Cross had shattered the dis-

[1] Mark 15. 34; Matt. 27. 46.

ciples' faith; 'we hoped'—but that is all over now—'we hoped that it was he which should redeem Israel.'[1] And their shattered faith was restored when the Risen Lord proved His conquest of death by appearing to those who loved Him and had believed in Him. So St Peter looked back to the first Easter as the day when not only the Lord, but also his own faith and hope were raised from the dead.[2] Our Lord, we notice, never appeared to Caiaphas or to any who had rejected Him. That would have been again to give the sign from heaven which might convince men against their will. But to those who had loved and believed He showed Himself, and to Thomas, utterly loyal,[3] but literal and unimaginative,[4] He offered the evidence he asked for.[5]

Indeed, if the Cross had been the end, then, so far at least as concerns the revelation offered to men, God would have failed Himself. We might still have hoped that the life of perfect love was continued somewhere beyond our vision or knowledge; but in just the same way we might have hoped that God is love even if the life of perfect love had not been lived. But it would have been a shadowy hope. If God is love, He must for His love's sake reveal His love; if He has not revealed it we hardly can dare to hope that He is love. Therefore the Incarnation is necessary to any sure faith in the love of God. But this means that we are to see in the story of Christ's earthly life the expression of the very Being of God; and if the story ends with the Cross it expresses anything but that. For by the Name

[1] Luke 24. 21.
[2] I Pet. 1. 3.
[3] John 11. 16.
[4] John 14. 5.
[5] John 20. 24-29.

of God we mean the perfect union of absolute power and absolute goodness. In the Life and Death of Christ without the Resurrection we see the perfect goodness, but if that is all, the power of the universe would seem to be against it. Only in the Resurrection is this union of absolute power and absolute goodness found. The Resurrection of Jesus Christ is more than the guarantee of His Messiahship; it is more than the pledge of our immortality; *it is the vindication of the Deity of God.*

(7) One more episode remains—*the Ascension.* Here, plainly, we have an acted parable. Our Lord, who after His Resurrection was able to appear among men as He would, was received up from them into the cloud of the divine glory.[1] I have no doubt that by the cloud here, as in the story of the Transfiguration,[2] we are to understand the Shekinah.[3]

Till then the Father was known, as He still is, only through the Son. But those who would be in the presence of the Son must go where He was to be found; it might be in Galilee, it might be in Jerusalem. But now this was so no longer. Jesus, and all that He means of Divine Love, is now wherever God is; and that is everywhere. *His Ascension means indeed the withdrawal of His bodily and local presence; but that is withdrawn only so that His spiritual presence may be everywhere available.* Because He is 'in heaven,' He is everywhere on earth; because He is ascended, He is here.

---

[1] Luke 24. 50-55; Acts 1. 9; Mark 16. 19.
[2] Mark 9. 7; Luke 9. 34, 35; Matt. 17. 5.
[3] Cf. e.g. I Kings 8. 10, 11.

We have completed our outline survey. I have not tried to argue or to meet difficulties, but merely to show you something of what I have found in Christ's revelation of God. There is much that may be said in argument, and it is right that we should try to understand as far as we may. But it is not chiefly by that method that we can test the truth of what has been before us; it is by the life of active and practical discipleship, in prayer and service. We shall find out whether these things are true if we take Him at His word when He says: 'If any man would come after me, let him deny himself and take up his cross and follow me', 'Come unto me, all ye that labour and are heavy laden, and I will give you rest.'